DESSERTS

DESSERTS
SPIRIT HOUSE

NEW
HOLLAND

CONTENTS

INTRODUCTION

Ask four Spirit House Restaurant chefs to choose their favourite desserts and the result is this pot pourri of sweet indulgences. Over 100 recipes, liberally sprinkled with chefs' tips on how to match tart flavours with sweet, how to counterbalance smooth textures with crunchy, or add an Asian twist to a traditional dessert classic. Plus the chefs show you how to create fantastic garnishes that will transform a simple cake or pudding into a dessert tour-de-force.

For summer entertaining, chill out with the recipes in the Ice section—a mixed bag of frozen and chilled delights to provide the coolest finish for the hottest party.

When autumn mists creep in, turn up the oven and fill your kitchen with warm baking aromas from the steamed puddings, tarts or cakes in Fire.

In Treats, you'll discover an eclectic range of bite-size temptations to serve with a pot of tea or an after-dinner coffee, while the section Bling contains, quite literally, the icing on the cake. There are a myriad of clever garnishing ideas and techniques to help create your own original 'dessert art'.

And when it's time to party, flick through to the back pages, because the Spirit House Bar staff have managed to sneak in a few of their favourite Cocktails—such an exotic way to kick-start a special celebration.

Sugar and spice—designed for each and every occasion.

Helen Brierty
(Owner)
Spirit House Restaurant and Cooking School

ICE

ANGLAISE ICE CREAM BASE

Makes about 600 ml
(18 fl oz)

250 ml (8½ fl oz) milk
250 ml (8½ fl oz) cream
1 vanilla bean
6 egg yolks
50 g (1¾ oz) caster
(superfine) sugar

Crème Anglaise is the ultimate pouring sauce to serve with many desserts. This Anglaise is also a base recipe for ice creams, but be careful to cook it on a low heat, otherwise it will curdle. ~ Nadine

Put milk and cream into a saucepan with the scraped vanilla bean, over a medium heat. Bring to the boil.

Whisk egg yolks and sugar until pale and creamy. Pour milk and cream mix onto the egg mix, whisking all the while.

Return mixture to the stove on a very low heat and cook until the mix thickens slightly and coats the back of a spoon. When you're able to draw a line with your finger along the back of your wooden spoon and the line remains distinct without liquid running into it for several seconds, the mixture is done.

Remove from the heat and strain through a fine sieve. Cover with cling film and cool.

CINNAMON ICE CREAM

Makes 1 litre (1¾ pints)

15 g (½ oz) whole cinnamon
    quill, slightly bashed
250 ml (8½ fl oz) milk
250 ml (8½ fl oz) cream
100 g (3½ oz) caster
    (superfine) sugar
5 egg yolks

Sweet and woody cinnamon brings a cosy warmth to this ice cream. Its aromatic fragrance embraces stone fruits like poached blood plums and melts into the heart of my Rhubarb, Apple and Ginger Crumble. ~ Libby

Combine the cinnamon, milk and cream in a saucepan. Place over a medium heat and bring to a simmer. Remove from heat and allow to sit aside for 20 minutes for the flavours to infuse. Return the saucepan to the heat and bring back to a simmer. Remove from the heat.

In a bowl, whisk the sugar into the egg yolks until pale and slightly thickened. Slowly pour the warm cinnamon milk mix into the egg mixture, whisking constantly.

Now place the bowl over a saucepan of simmering water, making sure the water level is well below the base of the bowl. Stir the egg mixture constantly and gently with a wooden spoon until the mixture begins to thicken. When you're able to draw a line with your finger along the back of your wooden spoon and the line remains distinct without liquid running into it for several seconds, the mixture is done.

Place the bowl inside a larger bowl filled with iced water; this will stop the cooking process. Stir frequently so the custard cools down evenly. Once cooled, strain the cinnamon out of the custard and churn in your ice cream machine as per the manufacturer's instructions.

Keep stored in your freezer in an airtight container.

CUSTARD APPLE ICE CREAM

Makes 1 litre (1¾ pints)

6 large egg yolks
200 g (7 oz) caster
   (superfine) sugar
200 ml (7 fl oz) milk
300 ml (10½ fl oz) clear
   custard apple juice (from
   fresh custard apples)
100 ml (3½ fl oz) single
   cream

I first made this as a challenge from a friend who wasn't fond of custard apple and defied me to make the fruit palatable. I served it simply with chocolate cake and some fresh berries. It went down a treat! ~ Nathan

Whisk the egg yolks and sugar together. Bring the milk to the boil and pour a little into the egg mixture while whisking, then add the rest of the milk and whisk. Pour the mixture into a stainless steel bowl and place on top of a pot of simmering water, stirring continuously until the mixture coats the back of a wooden spoon in a nice thick coating and doesn't run (approximately 10–15 minutes). Allow the mixture to cool over ice, stirring every now and then.

Meanwhile, using extremely ripe custard apples, scoop the flesh of approximately one large custard apple into a strainer lined with cheesecloth or a clean dishcloth. Gather the cloth at the top and squeeze the custard apple flesh tightly to obtain a clear juice.

When you have 300 ml (10½ fl oz) of clear juice whisk it into the custard with the 100 ml of single cream. Place the mixture into an ice cream churner and churn until ready. Place the ice cream in a container in the freezer until needed.

COCONUT RUM ICE CREAM

Makes about 700 ml
   (24 fl oz)

50 g (1¾ oz) desiccated
   coconut
300 ml (10½ fl oz) pouring
   cream
300 ml (10½ fl oz) milk
100 g (3½ oz) dark palm
   sugar, finely chopped
6 egg yolks
20 ml (²/3 fl oz) dark rum

This coconut rum ice cream can be served with summer fruits or with a sprinkling of crushed Coconut Meringue decorated with Chocolate Shards. ~ Nadine

Place coconut onto a baking tray and roast in a warm oven, at about 160°C (325°F), until golden.

Transfer coconut to a saucepan and add cream, milk, palm sugar.

Bring to a simmer for 1 minute.

Take off the heat and let stand for 10 minutes to infuse.

Whisk egg yolks, then slowly pour in the cream mixture. Return to a low heat, stirring continuously, until mixture coats the back of a spoon.

Strain through a fine sieve into a bowl placed over ice, stir in rum and cool completely. Place into ice cream machine, churn and freeze.

PALM SUGAR
& TAMARIND ICE CREAM

Makes 1 litre (1¾ pints)

375 g (13 oz) tamarind pulp
250 g (8½ oz) light palm
    sugar
5 egg yolks
500 ml (17 fl oz) cream

Here the sweetness of the palm sugar balances the sourness of the tamarind, leaving a unique fruit-flavoured, tangy ice cream. ~ Libby

Soak the tamarind pulp in a bowl with 1 litre (1¾ pints) of boiled water for 40 minutes. Every 10 minutes give the tamarind a good mash up with a whisk to help it disperse into the water. Strain tamarind water and discard solids. You will need to give it a good push through a sieve to extract all the liquid.

Measure 500 ml (17 fl oz) of the tamarind water, place in a saucepan and bring to a simmer. (Left-over tamarind water can be frozen down into ice cube trays, then added to curries when a sour flavour is needed.)

Finely grate the palm sugar into a bowl, add the egg yolks and whisk together until pale and slightly thickened. Slowly pour the tamarind water into the egg mixture, whisking constantly.

Place the bowl over a saucepan of simmering water, making sure the water level is well below the base of the bowl. Stir the egg mixture constantly and gently with a wooden spoon until the mixtures begins to thicken and you can draw a line with your finger along the back of your wooden spoon and the line remains distinct for several seconds.

Remove from heat and place the bowl inside a larger bowl filled with iced water; this will stop the cooking process. Stir frequently, until the mixture has cooled down.

Thoroughly stir in the cream and churn in your ice cream machine as per its manufacturer's instructions. Keep stored in your freezer in an airtight container.

DARK CHOCOLATE STAR ANISE ICE CREAM

Makes 1 litre (1¾ pints)

45 g (1½ oz) star anise, whole
125g (4 oz) dark chocolate, chopped
250 ml (8½ fl oz) milk
250 ml (8½ fl oz) cream
pinch salt
100 g (3½ oz) caster (superfine) sugar
5 yolks

Liquorice-flavoured, dark chocolate ice cream. If you enjoy chocolate-coated liquorice, you're going to love this ice cream. ~ Libby

In a 180°C (350°F) preheated oven, roast the star anise for 5 minutes. Allow to cool, then bash in half using a pestle and mortar.

Place the chocolate in a clean, dry bowl and place over a saucepan of simmering water, making sure the water level is well below the base of the bowl. Once the chocolate has melted, set it aside until needed.

Combine the star anise, milk, cream and salt in a saucepan. Place over a medium heat and bring to a simmer. Remove from heat and sit aside for 20 minutes for the flavours to infuse. Return the saucepan to the heat and return to simmer. Take off the heat, strain and discard the star anise.

In a bowl, whisk the sugar into the egg yolks. Slowly whisk in the warm milk mixture.

Place a bowl over a saucepan of simmering water. Stir the egg mixture constantly and gently with a wooden spoon until the mixtures begins to thicken and you can draw a line with your finger along the back of the spoon through the custard.

Remove from heat and stir the warm chocolate slowly into the warm custard mixture.

Place the bowl inside a larger bowl filled with iced water. Stir to cool the custard down. Churn in your ice cream machine as per its manufacturer's instructions. Keep stored in your freezer in an airtight container.

CHEAT'S BASIL ICE CREAM

Makes 500 ml (17½ fl oz)

100 g (3½ oz) caster
   (superfine) sugar
150 g (5 oz) water
12 large basil leaves
350 g (12 oz) good-quality
   vanilla ice cream (soften
   in refrigerator for half an
   hour)

This basil ice cream uses a cheat's method; simply use a good-quality, store-bought vanilla ice cream and jazz it up by adding a basil sugar syrup to it. Use the same amounts of sugar, water and ice cream, and then flavour it with your choice of herb, spice or aromatic. ~ Nathan

Boil the sugar and water until the sugar has dissolved, set aside to cool. Blanch the basil leaves in boiling water for 5–10 seconds and then place the leaves into some iced water to refresh. Drain well and place the basil leaves and the sugar syrup into a blender and process. Pass this mixture through a fine sieve and fold through the softened ice cream. Return the ice cream to the freezer until required.

HONEYCOMB RASPBERRY RIPPLE ICE CREAM

Makes 1 litre (1¾ pints)

HONEYCOMB
335 g (11¾ oz) caster
    (superfine) sugar
125 ml (4 fl oz) honey
80 ml (2½ fl oz) water
30 ml (1 fl oz) golden syrup
10 g (⅓ oz) bicarbonate of
    soda (baking soda)

ICE CREAM
250 ml (8½ fl oz) cream
250 ml (8½ fl oz) milk
100 g (3½ oz) caster
    (superfine) sugar
5 egg yolks
12 raspberries
12 honeycomb pieces,
    broken roughly into
    1 cm (½ in) sizes

Here's a smooth vanilla ice cream with chunks of crisp honeycomb and rippled hints of fruity raspberry sweetness. No matter what your age, this ice cream will thrill any child-at-heart. ~ Libby

Honeycomb
Line a tray with baking paper. In a saucepan, bring the sugar, honey, water and golden syrup to the boil over medium heat, without stirring, until the syrup reaches 154°C (309°F) on a sugar thermometer. Set aside.

Quickly whisk in the bicarbonate of soda—the hot mixture will now bubble and foam up. Pour this mixture onto the lined tray and allow to cool. Break the honeycomb down into manageable pieces and place in an airtight container. Store in the freezer for up to one month.

Ice Cream
Combine cream and milk in a saucepan and bring to a simmer. In a bowl, whisk the sugar into the egg yolks until slightly thickened. Slowly whisk the warm milk mixture into the egg mixture.

Place the bowl over a saucepan of simmering water, making sure the water level is well below the base of the bowl. Stir the egg mixture gently with a wooden spoon until it begins to thicken and you can draw a line with your finger along the back of your spoon. Remove from the heat. Place bowl inside a larger bowl filled with iced water and stir until cool. Churn in your ice cream machine as per its manufacturer's instructions.

Once ice cream has finished churning, add the raspberry and honeycomb pieces and allow to churn a few more turns to create a rippled effect. Keep stored in freezer in an airtight container.

SPICED ICE CREAM

Makes just under 500 ml
(17½ fl oz)

400 ml (14 fl oz) pure cream
1 vanilla bean, whole
½ teaspoon ground
cinnamon
½ teaspoon ground ginger
¼ teaspoon ground nutmeg
¼ teaspoon ground
cardamom
¼ teaspoon ground
star anise
2 egg yolks
85 g (3 oz) caster (superfine)
sugar

A taste of the Spice Islands! Serve this subtly spiced ice cream with tropical fruits or with my Orange Cake and Citrus Syrup. ~ Renee

Heat cream, vanilla and spices to just before a simmer, then set aside to infuse for 30 minutes.

Whisk egg yolks and sugar together, add spiced cream mixture. Cook mix over a double boiler (making sure the water doesn't touch the bottom of the bowl) until it thickens to a spoon-coating consistency.

Strain mix and sit bowl in an ice bath to cool.

Churn mix in ice cream, then store in freezer. Or place mix in freezer, whisking every 15 minutes until frozen.

VANILLA & BLACK PEPPER ICE CREAM

Makes 500 ml (17½ fl oz)

10 g (⅓ oz) black
   peppercorns
250 ml (8½ fl oz) milk
250 ml (8½ fl oz) cream
2 vanilla beans, split
   lengthwise
5 egg yolks
100 g (3½ oz) caster
   (superfine) sugar

This creamy vanilla bean ice cream has a surprising black peppercorn flavour that sneaks up on you and is a perfect accompaniment for my Pineapple Tarte Tatin. ~ Libby

Place the peppercorns into a pestle and mortar and coarsely grind.

Combine the milk, cream, vanilla beans and ground pepper into a saucepan over a medium heat and bring to a simmer. Remove from heat and set aside for 20 minutes for the flavours to infuse. Return to heat and bring back to a simmer.

In a bowl, whisk together the egg yolks and sugar, then slowly whisk in the warm milk.

Place the bowl over a saucepan of simmering water, making sure the water level is well below the base of the bowl. Stir the egg mixture constantly and gently with a wooden spoon until the mixture begins to thicken and you can draw a line with your finger along the back of your wooden spoon through the custard.

Remove custard from heat and place the bowl inside a larger bowl filled with iced water. Stir to cool down. Strain the custard to remove the pepper and vanilla beans. Churn in an ice cream machine as per its manufacturer's instructions. Keep stored in an airtight container in the freezer.

SALTED PISTACHIO ICE CREAM SANDWICH

Makes 18 sandwiches

SABLE BISCUITS

260 g (9 oz) softened
   unsalted butter
75 g (2½ oz) icing
   (confectioners') sugar
1 small egg (lightly beaten)
250 g (9 oz) plain (all-
   purpose) flour
50 g (1¾ oz) cocoa powder
75 g (2¾ oz) almond meal

I love this ice cream so I couldn't pass up the opportunity to use it in an ice cream sandwich on a recent Spirit House menu. As with all of these recipes, don't be afraid to put your own spin on it. The sable biscuit can be used as a base recipe; just add your own favourite ice cream. ~ Nathan

Sable Biscuits

Cream together the butter and the icing sugar then beat in the egg. Sift the flour, cocoa powder and almond meal together and add to the creamed mixture. Bring together to form a dough, but be careful not to overwork it. Place the dough onto a large sheet of baking paper and place another large sheet of baking paper over the top. Using a rolling pin, roll the dough out to about ½ cm (¼ in) thick. Place the rolled out dough, still in the paper, onto a flat tray and refrigerate for at least an hour, or even overnight.

Once you are ready to bake, preheat oven to 180°C (350°F). Remove the top layer of baking paper and prick well with a fork. Cut out 36 circles using a 7.5 cm (3 in) ring cutter, or if preferred, just cut them to even sizes with a knife. A ruler should be used to ensure they are all the same size. Place onto a baking tray lined with baking paper and bake for 20 minutes, until crisp. Leave to cool on the tray. Once cool, store in an airtight container until ready to use.

SALTED PISTACHIO ICE CREAM

1 egg white

250 g (9 oz) salted and
   shelled pistachio nuts

600 ml (20 fl oz) double
   cream

400 ml (14 fl oz) full cream
   milk

12 medium egg yolks

250 g (9 oz) caster (superfine)
   sugar

Salted Pistachio Ice Cream

Preheat the oven to 180°C (350°F). Whisk the egg white by hand until it makes a light foam. Take a tablespoon of the foam and mix it with the pistachio nuts—should be enough to coat them lightly. Spread the nuts over a baking tray lined with baking paper and bake for 5 minutes until they dry out but don't discolour. Leave them to cool, then chop finely.

Bring the cream and milk to the boil. Mix the egg yolks together in a large bowl. Pour the cream and milk onto the egg and sugar mixture in a steady stream and stir well. Return the mixture to a clean pan and cook over a low heat, stirring constantly with a wooden spoon, making sure to get into the edges so that the custard doesn't catch. Keep stirring until the mixture thickens enough to coat the back of a spoon: it should register 86°C (185°F) on a sugar thermometer if you have one. Do not let it boil or the custard will separate.

Pass immediately through a fine sieve into a bowl and stir in the pistachio nuts Place into the refrigerator to cool completely.

If you have an ice cream churner you can churn it and then place into a tray lined with baking paper (will work better this way). If not, you can just place the ice cream into a tray lined with baking paper and set it in the freezer. You want a depth of about 2.5 cm (1 in) for your ice cream. Once you have set it in the freezer, use a ring cutter or knife to cut the desired shape of ice cream.

Sandwich the ice cream between the sable biscuits and serve. If you like, put a little melted chocolate or ganache onto the inner side of the sable biscuits and this will help the sandwich layers stay together.

BASE SORBET SUGAR SYRUP

Makes 1 litre (1¾ pints)

600 ml (21 fl oz) water
400 g (14 oz) caster
    (superfine) sugar
100 g (3½ oz) glucose syrup

Refreshing sorbets are perfect for summer and are a wonderful low-fat alternative to ice cream. This sorbet base recipe is quick and easy to make. Just add your favourite pureed fruit, or a splash of alcohol for an adult icy treat. ~ Libby

Place all ingredients into a large saucepan, over a medium heat. Allow the mix to slowly come to the simmer, stir well, then remove from the heat. Cool down and keep covered in the refrigerator until needed.

TIP
The important thing to remember when serving sorbet is to remove it from the freezer five minutes before you actually need it. Doing this will slightly warm and melt the sorbet, giving it a much softer and smoother consistency.

MANGO & CHILLI SORBET

Makes 2 litres (70 fl oz)

500 ml (17 fl oz) base sorbet
    sugar syrup (see recipe)
1 red birds eye chilli,
    chopped
900 ml (30½ fl oz) mango
    puree, sieved
100 ml (2¾ fl oz) coconut
    cream
200 ml (7 fl oz) lime juice

Luscious mango, creamy coconut and a hint of spicy chilli combine here for a delightful tropical refreshment. ~ Libby

Place sugar syrup and chopped chilli into saucepan and heat to simmer. Remove from heat, stir in mango puree, coconut cream and lime juice until well incorporated. Strain out chilli and cool down in the refrigerator before churning in an ice cream machine as per the manufacturer's instructions. Store sorbet in an airtight container in the freezer.

RASPBERRY & MINT SORBET

Makes 500 ml (17½ fl oz)

500 ml (17½ fl oz) base
    sorbet sugar syrup
    (see recipe)
500 g (17½ oz) frozen
    raspberries
60 g (2 oz) mint leaves

Gorgeously pink, with bold, intense raspberries and fresh mint, this sorbet tastes just as lovely as it looks. ~ Libby

Place the sugar syrup and raspberries into a saucepan and heat to a simmer. Remove from heat and add the mint leaves. Allow this mix to cool down to room temperature. Once cooled, blend with an electric blender and then strain to remove the mint and raspberry seeds. Chill the mix down in the refrigerator before churning in an ice cream machine as per the manufacturer's instructions. Store the sorbet in an airtight container in the freezer.

LYCHEE & LIME SORBET

Makes 1 litre (1¾ pints)

2 x 567 g (20 oz) cans
   lychees
500 ml (17 fl oz) base sorbet
   sugar syrup (see recipe)
400 ml (14 fl oz) lime juice

This sweet lychee and sour lime sorbet is a wonderfully refreshing icy cold treat. Try this palate-cleansing sorbet between savoury courses, at the end of a meal or straight from the freezer on a hot day. ~ Libby

With electric blender, blend together entire contents of both lychee cans. Strain the liquid to remove pulp. Combine lychee liquid with sugar syrup and lime juice. Chill mix in the refrigerator before churning in an ice cream machine as per the manufacturer's instructions. Store sorbet in an airtight container in freezer.

DARK CHOCOLATE & PASSIONFRUIT SORBET

Makes 1 litre (1¾ pints)

500 ml (17 fl oz) base sorbet
    sugar syrup (see recipe)
50 g (1¾ oz) cocoa powder
250 ml (8 fl oz) passionfruit
    pulp
pinch salt
120 g (4 oz) dark chocolate,
    chopped

Here the dark chocolate brings a lovely creamy texture to this sorbet and the passionfruit brings an intense, aromatic, tart surprise. ~ Libby

Place sugar syrup, cocoa powder, passionfruit pulp and salt into a saucepan over medium heat. Whisk together and allow the mix to come to a simmer. Remove from heat and strain out the passionfruit seeds. Add chocolate pieces and stir well until all dissolved. Chill the mix down in the refrigerator before churning in ice cream machine as per the manufacturer's instructions. Store the sorbet in an airtight container in the freezer.

LEMON & BASIL SORBET

Makes 1 litre (1¾ pints)

500 ml (17 fl oz) base sorbet
    sugar syrup (see recipe)
60 g (2 oz) basil leaves
400 ml (14 fl oz) lemon juice

Lemony freshness combined with beautifully perfumed basil enlivens this sorbet. ~ Libby

Place the sugar syrup in a saucepan over medium heat and bring to a simmer. Remove from heat and add the basil leaves. Allow this mix to cool down to room temperature.

Add lemon juice and blend with an electric blender. Strain mix and chill down in the refrigerator before churning in an ice cream machine as per the manufacturer's instructions.

Store the sorbet in an airtight container in the freezer.

MINT SORBET

Makes about 1 litre (1¾ pints)

250 ml (8½ fl oz) lime juice
    (about 8–10 limes)
250 ml (8½ fl oz) base sorbet
    sugar syrup (see recipe)
350 ml (11¾ fl oz) water
1 large bunch mint, leaves
    only
125 ml (4¼ fl oz)
    crème de menthe

This really is a great adult sorbet. It's so irresistibly fresh and light and the taste is amazing. Do be cautious though because it still contains the alcohol content, as it hasn't been cooked out, so probably best to keep this one a secret from the kids. ~ Nathan

Place the lime juice, sugar syrup, water and mint into a saucepan and bring to the boil. Simmer for 2–3 minutes, take off the heat and let steep to infuse while it completely cools. Pour through a fine strainer to remove the mint leaves. Stir the crème de menthe into the infused syrup. Pour into an ice cream maker and churn until almost firm. Transfer to a plastic airtight container and freeze.

TIP
If you would like to colour this sorbet green, add some food colouring until you reach the desired shade. For the best texture, use sorbet on the same day it is made. Alternatively, melt the sorbet and re-churn it.

COCONUT GINGER SORBET

Makes about 700 ml
(24 fl oz)

250 ml (8½ fl oz) base sorbet
sugar syrup (see recipe)
5 g (¼ oz) ground ginger
half vanilla bean, split and
scraped
⅛ teaspoon (2 pinches) salt
300 ml (10½ fl oz) coconut
cream
45 g (1½ oz) shredded
coconut, toasted

*This sorbet is beautifully creamy and fresh on the
palate, perfect for summer entertaining. ~ Nadine*

Place sugar syrup, ginger, vanilla and salt in saucepan
and slowly bring up to simmer.
  Take off heat, strain and add coconut cream.
  Cool and churn in ice cream machine.
  Serve with fresh tropical fruits such mango, banana
or papaya in long glass and garnish sorbet with toasted
shredded coconut.

WATERMELON GRANITA

Makes 500 ml (17½ fl oz)

1 kg (2 lb 4 oz) watermelon,
  roughly chopped
30 g (1 oz) caster (superfine)
  sugar
30 ml (1 fl oz) vodka

This granita is very quick to make so is a good option if you are short of time. The only issue with granita is that it will quickly turn to liquid, so serve it at once for the 'wow' factor. On the upside, it does have vodka in it! ~ Nathan

Blitz the watermelon, sugar and the vodka to a fine liquid in a food processor. Pass the liquid through a sieve into a shallow plastic tray and freeze until required. Use a fork to scrape the frozen granita into crystals and serve immediately.

LEMONGRASS GRANITA

Makes 500 ml (17½ fl oz)

500 ml (17½ fl oz) water
125 g (4 oz) caster
    (superfine) sugar
3 tablespoons (45 g) glucose
    syrup
1 lemon, juice only (peel
    skin off lemon before
    juicing and save skin to
    make Lemon Candy (see
    recipe)
4 lemongrass stalks (roughly
    chopped)
1 lime, zest only

Spoon into a martini glass with summer fruits; this is delicious served with my Deconstructed Citrus Pistachio Tart. ~ Nadine

Heat water, sugar and glucose in a heavy-based saucepan until sugar has dissolved.
    Increase heat and boil for 3 minutes.
    Take off the heat and stir in lemon juice, lemongrass and lime zest. Set aside to infuse until cold.
    Strain the syrup, pour into shallow freezer container and freeze until almost cold.
    Scrape lightly with a fork 2–3 times as it freezes. You should have a snow effect.

FROZEN CARAMEL PARFAIT,
peanut popcorn crunch & chocolate vanilla sauce

Serves 6

Creamy caramel, crisp popcorn, crunchy peanut and smooth chocolate join together in delightful decadence. ~ Libby

CHOCOLATE VANILLA SAUCE
40 g (1½ oz) corn syrup
20 ml (2/3 fl oz) vegetable oil
1 vanilla bean, split
    lengthwise
10 g (1/3 oz) caster
    (superfine) sugar
110 ml (3½ fl oz) cream
150 g (5 oz) dark chocolate,
    chopped
50 ml (1¾ fl oz) milk

PEANUT POPCORN CRUNCH
40 g (1½ oz) popcorn,
    already prepared
35 g (1¼ oz) peanuts,
    chopped
60 g (2 oz) brown sugar
10 g (1/3 oz) salt
45 ml (1½ fl oz) vegetable oil
45 ml (1½ fl oz) corn syrup
½ lime, zest
pinch bicarbonate of soda
    (baking soda)

Chocolate Vanilla Sauce

Place corn syrup, oil, vanilla bean, sugar and 55 ml (1¾ fl oz) of cream into a saucepan. Bring to a simmer over medium heat.

Place chocolate into bowl and pour over the warm cream mixture.

Whisk in the milk and the remaining 55 ml (1¾ fl oz) of cream. Stir well to combine. Strain and cool. Keep stored in an airtight container in the refrigerator.

Popcorn Peanut Crunch

Preheat oven to 120°C (250°F) and line an oven tray with baking paper.

Place the popcorn and peanuts into a bowl.

Combine the sugar, salt, oil and corn syrup in a small saucepan and place over a medium heat. Bring to the boil and stir for 5 minutes until nice and thick.

Remove from heat and add lime zest and pinch of bicarbonate of soda. Stir the mixture as it is bubbling up and pour it over the popcorn and peanut mix. Stir to coat well.

Transfer to baking tray and bake for 30 minutes, or until nicely browned. Remove from oven, allow to cool and become crisp on the tray. Keep stored in an airtight container, away from moisture for 1 week.

FROZEN CARAMEL PARFAIT

125 ml (4 fl oz) milk
125 ml (4 fl oz) cream
115 g (4 oz) caster (superfine)
    sugar
8 egg yolks
60 g (2 oz) caster (superfine)
    sugar
1 vanilla bean, split
    lengthwise
250 ml (8 fl oz) cream
10g (1/3 oz) icing
    (confectioners') sugar

Frozen Caramel Parfait

Combine the milk and cream in a saucepan and bring to a boil over medium heat.

Place a heavy-based saucepan over medium heat and add 1 tablespoon of the 115 g (4 oz) of sugar.

Once the sugar melts, sprinkle in remaining sugar. Stir until the caramel begins to darken and slightly smoke, then pour over warm milk mix—the mixture will now bubble and spit at you. Stir until lump free and remove from heat.

Whisk together the egg yolks and 60g (2 oz) of sugar until pale and slightly thickened. Slowly pour in the warm caramel mix.

Place the bowl over a saucepan of simmering water, making sure the water level is below the base of the bowl. Stir the egg mixture constantly and gently with a wooden spoon until the mixture begins to thicken and you can draw a line with your finger along the back of wooden spoon through the custard.

Remove from the heat and strain into the bowl of an electric mixer. Beat on high for 10 minutes, or until mix is completely cool. Transfer to a large bowl.

Whisk the remaining 250 ml (8 fl oz) of cream until it holds soft peaks. Fold into the caramel custard mix.

Pour the parfait mix into eight 125ml (4 fl oz) dariole moulds, lightly sprayed with non-stick spray. Place in the freezer and allow to set overnight.

To Serve

Dip the dariole mould into hot water for a few seconds to soften the parfait edges. Run a small knife around the inside of each mould and turn out onto serving plate. Place the peanut popcorn crunch atop and to the side of each parfait and dust with the icing sugar. Drizzle over the chocolate and vanilla sauce.

CHOCOLATE, ORANGE & STAR ANISE PARFAIT
with pistachio praline

Serve 9

CHOCOLATE, ORANGE & STAR ANISE PARFAIT

3 eggs, yolks and whites
   separated
120 g (4 oz) caster
   (superfine) sugar
30 ml (1 fl oz) Grand Marnier
   orange liqueur
110 g (3½ oz) dark
   chocolate, chopped
150 ml (5 fl oz) pure cream
1½ teaspoons finely ground
   star anise

CHOCOLATE BISCUIT BASE

65g (2 oz) unsalted butter
80 g (2½ oz) brown sugar
1 egg
120 g (4 oz) plain (all-
   purpose) flour
20 g (²/3 oz) self-raising (self-
   rising) flour
20 g (²/3 oz) cocoa powder

This is a deliciously rich dessert—but it is the perfect end to a summer meal and can easily be made gluten-free by removing the biscuit base. ~ Renee

Chocolate, Orange & Star Anise Parfait

With your mixer on high, whisk egg yolks, sugar and Grand Marnier liqueur until pale and thick. You should be able to drizzle some mixture off the whisk and it will sit on top briefly before sinking into the mix.

Melt chocolate over double boiler. When completely melted, set aside to cool.

Whip cream to soft peaks. Whip egg whites to soft peaks. Fold whipped cream and star anise into egg yolk mix. Quickly fold in cooled melted chocolate. Finally fold in whipped egg whites. Pour into an 18 cm (7 in) square tin lined with baking paper and freeze.

Chocolate Biscuit Base

Whisk butter and sugar until light and fluffy, then beat in egg.

Sift both flours and cocoa powder then add to mixer on a slow speed, in two batches, mixing until just combined.

Turn mix onto floured surface and knead until smooth.

Roll the mix between baking paper until it is 2–3 cm (¾–1 in) thick, then rest in refrigerator for at least 30 minutes.

Cook on a square tray larger than 18 cm (7 in), line with baking paper and bake at 180°C (350°F) for 12–15 minutes until cooked.

When the base comes out of the oven, take the parfait

ORANGE GARNISH

1 orange

PISTACHIO PRALINE GARNISH

1 quantity Pistachio Praline
(see recipe)

from the freezer and turn it out onto the base. The heat from the biscuit base will melt the parfait slightly and join them together. Return it to the freezer to reset.

When completely set, remove from freezer and using a hot sharp knife (run knife under hot water to heat) trim up the edges and slice into 9 portions. Store in airtight container in freezer until ready to serve.

Orange Garnish

Peel one orange, removing all the white bits, then using a small knife, slice on either side of the membrane to the centre of orange. Continue all the way around cutting the orange into segments.

Pistachio Praline Garnish

Make the Pistachio Praline to garnish your dessert.

To Serve

Remove parfait from freezer, arrange parfait slices on individual serving plates. Scatter a couple of orange segments on the top and sides, then sprinkle Pistachio Praline on top, plus a little around the side of the plates.

MANGO & PASSIONFRUIT PARFAIT
with white chocolate anglaise

Serves 8

Light and tropical ... a perfect end to a summer dinner. ~ Nadine

PÂTÉ À BOMBE

5 large egg yolks
150 g (5oz) caster (superfine) sugar
100 ml (3½ fl oz) water

MANGO & PASSIONFRUIT PARFAIT

2 large ripe mangoes
3 ripe passionfruit
2 large free-range egg whites
squeeze of lemon juice
100 g (3½ oz) caster (superfine) sugar
250 ml (8½ fl oz) double cream
1 quantity Pâté à Bombe

Pâté à Bombe

Place the egg yolks in a heat-proof bowl and whisk until pale, thick and creamy.

Heat the sugar with 100 ml (3½ fl oz) of water in a small saucepan until sugar dissolves,

Turn the heat to high and boil sugar syrup for 4–5 minutes until the edges start to turn golden.

Pour the sugar syrup gradually into the pale yolk mixture, whisking until you have a pale light foam.

Mango & Passionfruit Parfait

Peel and cut the mangoes—you should have about 350 g (12 oz) of mango flesh.

Place mango into a blender along with the passionfruit pulp, then put through a sieve and chill.

Whisk the egg whites and lemon juice in a bowl until stiff, then gradually whisk in the sugar, until you have a glossy meringue.

Whip the cream in another bowl until soft peaks form.

Fold the chilled fruit into the Pâté à Bombe mixture.

Then fold this mixture into the meringue, and finally fold in the whipped cream. Spoon mixture into eight individual moulds and freeze until firm.

WHITE CHOCOLATE ANGLAISE

1 quantity Anglaise Ice
    Cream Base (see recipe)
200 g (7 oz) white chocolate,
    melted

TO SERVE

fresh raspberries
orange segments
micro mint

White Chocolate Anglaise

Make up the Anglaise Ice Cream Base recipe.

While the Anglaise is still warm, whisk in the melted white chocolate. Strain the mixture.

To Serve

Unmould parfaits straight onto serving plates. Spoon the White Chocolate Anglaise around the parfait.

Decorate with fresh raspberries, orange segments and micro mint scattered around the plate.

A Pineapple Swizzle Stick (see recipe) would also make an unusual garnish.

COCONUT RICE MOUSSE, MANGO JELLY,
pineapple & mint compote

Serves 6

COCONUT RICE MOUSSE

1 gelatine sheet
1 teaspoon water, to soak
    the gelatine
70 g (2½ oz) jasmine rice
1 vanilla bean (halved and
    scraped)
185 ml (6½ fl oz) cream
185 ml (6½ fl oz) milk
75 g (2¾ oz) light palm sugar
50 g (1¾ oz) caster
    (superfine) sugar
25 g (¾ oz) coconut milk
    powder
185 ml (6½ fl oz) extra cream
    (whipped to soft peaks)

MANGO JELLY

1 quantity Mango Jelly (see
    recipe)

This takes a little time to prepare but is definitely worth the effort—it looks beautiful served in individual dessert glasses. ~ Nadine

Coconut Rice Mousse
Soak gelatine sheet in water. Rinse rice well under cold water.

Put rice, vanilla bean and seeds, cream, milk , sugars and coconut milk powder into a pot and bring to a simmer.

Reduce heat and cook for 20–25 minutes, stirring occasionally until the rice absorbs the liquid but still has a bite (not soft). Remove from heat. Add gelatine and liquid and mix well. Remove vanilla bean.

Cool mix, then fold in extra whipped cream.

Pour into a lamington tray or a tray about 25 cm (9¾ in) x 15 cm (6 in) lined with baking paper. Smooth surface with palette knife and freeze until firm.

Mango Jelly
Make Mango Jelly according to the recipe.

PINEAPPLE & MINT COMPOTE

50 g (1¾ oz) pineapple
    cubes cut into 1 cm (½ in)
    pieces
20 g (²/3 oz) light palm sugar
    finely grated bunch

TO SERVE

micro mint or mint leaves,
    finely chopped

Pineapple & Mint Compote

Mix pineapple and palm sugar together. Let pineapple sit for 1 hour, mixing occasionally. This will ensure the sugar has dissolved.

To Serve

Have a bowl of hot water ready. Place cookie cutters (4 x 4 cm/1¾ x 1¾ in or desired size) into hot water which will give a clean finish on the edges. Press down with even pressure onto the mousse to cut into shape.

Cut Mango Jelly with the same shape cutter, but this time make sure the cutter is clean and dry.

Place mousse on plate, top with jelly square.

Garnish with Pineapple & Mint Compote and place a small amount on top of jelly. Garnish with micro mint or finely chopped mint leaves.

FROZEN DARK CHOCOLATE, RASPBERRY, CHILLI MOUSSE CAKE, HONEYCOMB PIECES, RASPBERRY DUST

& honeycomb raspberry ripple ice cream

Serves 6

DARK CHOCOLATE, RASPBERRY, CHILLI MOUSSE CAKE

450 g (1 lb) dark chocolate pieces
125 g (4 oz) unsalted butter, diced
2 birds eye chillies, chopped
200 g (7 oz) raspberries
5 eggs
60 g (2 oz) caster (superfine) sugar
30 g (1 oz) plain (all-purpose) flour

It's a chocolate cake, with a difference. It's also part mousse! This is stored in the freezer, but served at room temperature. The cake is cooked on a high heat for a short time so the centre remains lovely and light. The added chilli leaves a lingering heat to this chilled treat. ~ Libby

Dark Chocolate, Raspberry and Chilli Mousse Cake
Preheat the oven to 250°C (485°F). Line a 20 cm (8 in) cake tin with baking paper and spray with oil.

Combine the chocolate, butter, chillies and raspberries in a bowl. Place bowl over a saucepan of simmering water, making sure the water level is well below the base of the bowl. Stir until chocolate and butter have melted. Remove from heat and strain out chilli and raspberry seeds.

In another bowl, beat the eggs and sugar over a saucepan of simmering water until sugar has dissolved. Remove from the heat and pour into an electric mixer and whisk on a high speed for 15 minutes. The mixture will more than double in size.

Fold through the sifted flour. Fold one-third of the egg mixture into the chocolate and mix thoroughly. Follow with the next third, then the last third, being careful to not lose too much air volume from the egg mixture.

TO SERVE

15 g (½ oz) icing
   (confectioners') sugar
24 raspberries
24 small honeycomb
   pieces (see recipe for
   Honeycomb Raspberry
   Ripple Ice Cream)
1 quantity Raspberry Dust
   (see recipe)
1 quantity Honeycomb
   Raspberry Ripple Ice
   Cream (see recipe)

Once well combined, pour mixture into your prepared cake tin and bake for only 20 minutes.

Remove cake from oven and allow to cool in the cake tin.

Once the cake has cooled, wrap the whole cake, tin and all, tightly in cling film and freeze for at least 24 hours.

To Serve

Transfer the cake to the refrigerator for 20 minutes prior to serving. This slightly defrosts the cake's edges, which makes portioning easier. Cut six portions, using a knife that has been dipped into hot water and wiped dry. The remaining cake can be rewrapped, returned to the freezer, and kept stored for up to one month.

Dust the top of each mousse cake portion with icing sugar and place each into the centre of your six serving places. Place four raspberries and four small honeycomb pieces around the plate at the base of each mousse cake. Dust these with Raspberry Dust. Top the mousse cake with a large scoop of Honeycomb Raspberry Ripple Ice Cream and serve immediately.

WHITE CHOCOLATE CHAI MOUSSE
with lemongrass ginger biscuit & candied banana

Serves 6

WHITE CHOCOLATE CHAI MOUSSE

120 ml (4 fl oz) pure cream
60 g (2 oz) white chocolate
1 egg yolk
15 g (½ oz) icing
   (confectioners') sugar
2 teaspoons chai syrup

TO SERVE

12–18 pieces Candied
   Banana (see recipe)
1 quantity Lemongrass
   Ginger Biscuits (see
   recipe)

Chai syrup is based on an Indian sweetened spiced tea predominantly flavoured with ginger, cardamom, cinnamon, cloves. When pregnant, I was often caught at the refrigerator indulging my sweet cravings with this creamy chai mousse.
~ Renee

White Chocolate Chai Mousse

Put 25 ml (¾ fl oz) of cream and white chocolate in a heat-proof bowl. Place bowl over a saucepan of water, heat until water boils then remove from heat and gently stir until the chocolate has all melted. Place back on heat if not completely melted.

Whisk egg yolk and icing sugar until pale, then cook over a low heat until thickened.

Strain yolk mix through a fine strainer, then cool slightly.

Fold chocolate mix through yolk mix, then add chai syrup.

Whip the rest of the cream to soft peaks then gently fold through cooled chocolate mix, one-third at a time

Fill six 80 ml (3 fl oz) glasses or Chinese tea cups with mousse and refrigerate until set—approximately 1–2 hours.

To Serve

Place mousse on desired serving plate, top with 2–3 slices of Candied Banana.

Dust Lemongrass Ginger Biscuits with icing sugar and serve a couple on the side of the mousse.

CHOCOLATE CHILLI MOUSSE

Serves 6

135 ml (4 fl oz) milk
2 long red chillies
2 egg yolks
35 g (1¼ oz) sugar
95 g (3½ oz) dark chocolate
100 ml (3½ fl oz) cream
1 quantity Raspberry
    Champagne Jelly (see
    recipe), garnish

Chocolate with a subtle hot kick. Garnish with some cooling cubes of Raspberry Champagne Jelly, or for ultimate decadence, serve with my Flourless Chocolate Cake. ~ Renee

Put milk and chillies in a saucepan, heat to just before boiling stage. Set aside and allow to infuse for 30 minutes.

Whisk egg yolks and sugar together, add infused milk.

Melt chocolate in a double boiler, making sure the water doesn't touch the bottom of the bowl.

Cook milk mixture over a double boiler until it thickens to spoon-coating consistency, stirring continually.

Strain mix, discarding the chillies.

Add melted chocolate and allow to cool slightly.

Whip the cream, fold cream into chocolate mix. Pour into six individual glasses or one large glass serving bowl.

Store in refrigerator until needed. Garnish each glass with cubes of Raspberry Champagne Jelly.

PINEAPPLE RAVIOLI
with lemon basil mousse

Serves 10–12

PINEAPPLE RAVIOLI
200 ml (7 fl oz) sugar syrup
200 ml (7 fl oz) water
30 ml (1 fl oz) Malibu (white
  rum)
juice of half a lemon
1 vanilla bean, split and
  seeds removed (reserve
  seeds for the mousse)
1 large ripe pineapple

ITALIAN MERINGUE
50 g (1¾ oz) caster
  (superfine) sugar
1 tablespoon water
1 teaspoon glucose syrup
1 large egg white

This dessert is stunning and has endless possibilities for fillings—ice cream, sorbet, mousse, jelly or even a flavoured cream. Here I have filled it with Lemon Basil Mousse which, in my opinion, is a flavour match made in heaven. This mousse recipe makes more than is needed, but is so yummy served by itself.
~ Nathan

Pineapple Ravioli
Pour the sugar syrup and water into a medium saucepan, add the rum, lemon juice and vanilla bean. Bring to boil and slightly reduce for 5 minutes.

Transfer to a large bowl and leave to cool.

To prepare the pineapple, cut off the base and top, stand fruit upright on chopping board. Slice off the skin following the natural curve of the pineapple. Pry out any remaining eyes with the tip of the knife. Now turn the pineapple on its side and cut 16–24 very thin slices using a long serrated knife. Place the slices into the cooled syrup as you cut them, making sure that each slice is separated and well coated with syrup before adding the next slice. Cover the bowl with cling film and place in the refrigerator overnight to soften the pineapple slices.

Italian Meringue
Put the sugar, water and glucose in a saucepan and stir over a low heat until the sugar has dissolved. Once the liquid is clear, increase the heat and boil for 4–6 minutes or until the temperature reaches 120°C (250°F).

Whisk the egg white to a soft peak using an electric beater. Slowly trickle the hot liquid onto the egg white,

LEMON BASIL MOUSSE

2 ripe mangoes

2 titanium gelatine sheets
(see Glossary)

50 g (1½ oz) caster
(superfine) sugar

150 ml (5 fl oz) lemon juice
(about 4 lemons)

10 large basil leaves

200 ml (7 fl oz) double cream

whisking all the time. Keep whisking for 5 minutes until meringue is firm, white and glossy and the bowl is no longer hot. Cover with cling film and set aside.

Lemon Basil Mousse

Peel the mangoes and dice into small pieces (about 5 mm/1/8 in). Set aside. Soak the gelatine in cold water for a few minutes to soften.

Put the sugar, lemon juice and reserved vanilla seeds into a small saucepan and stir over a low heat until the sugar has dissolved.

Bring to the boil and place into a large bowl. Drain the gelatine and squeeze out as much excess water as possible. Add the gelatine to the hot lemon syrup, stirring to dissolve. Leave to cool, stirring occasionally.

When the lemon syrup has cooled, fold it through the cream. Finely slice the basil and fold the basil and mango into the meringue mixture. Cover with cling film and refrigerate for no less than a couple of hours.

To Serve

Pat each slice of pineapple dry with paper towel. Separate slices into smallest and largest pieces. Use the smallest for the base of the ravioli and the largest for the top.

Place a small slice of pineapple onto a serving plate. With an ice cream scoop, scoop a round ball of the mousse mixture and place onto the pineapple slice. Get a large pineapple slice and place over the mousse and press the pineapple slices together around the mousse to make your ravioli. Drizzle some of the pineapple marinating syrup over the ravioli and garnish with your choice of diced fruits.

RASPBERRY CHAMPAGNE JELLY

Makes 500 ml (17½ fl oz)

350 g (11½ oz) fresh
    raspberries (frozen are
    fine to use)
50 g (1½ oz) caster
    (superfine) sugar
200 ml (7 fl oz) water
200 ml (7 fl oz) champagne
4½ leaf gelatine sheets

I use jellies as often as possible, not just in desserts but often in place of sauce. They add an extra dimension to a dish. This is a basic jelly recipe that you can use with any number of different ingredients, especially any in-season berry. ~ Nathan

Place the raspberries, sugar, water and Champagne into a pan and bring the ingredients to a simmer. Once simmering, place the mix into a food processor and blitz until smooth.

Meanwhile, soak the gelatine in some cold water for about 5 minutes.

Pass the berry mixture through a fine sieve into a bowl to remove the seeds. Remove the gelatine from the water and squeeze out any excess water. Place the gelatine into the raspberry mixture and stir well to dissolve the gelatine. Pass through a fine sieve again to remove any remaining seeds and un-dissolved gelatine.

Line a shallow tray or container with cling film and pour in the jelly; the cling film will make it easy to get the jelly out of the container so you can cut it into your desired shapes and sizes. Set the jelly in the refrigerator and then cut it into cubes, slices or rounds. Place it back into the refrigerator until ready to serve.

TIP

If you don't want to use Champagne you must replace it with an equal amount of liquid. Water, rosé, Prosecco or a nice dessert wine would be suitable, but you may have to alter the sugar to taste.

MANGO JELLY

Makes 350 ml (12 fl oz)

3 titanium gelatine sheets
250 g (9 oz) mango puree
100 ml (2¾ fl oz) cold water
25 g (¾ oz) caster (superfine)
   sugar

Serve with my Coconut Rice Mousse. Or set some jelly in the bottom third of a tall glass, add some diced tropical fruits and top with a scoop of Coconut Rum Ice Cream. ~ Nadine

Soak gelatine in cold water.

Heat mango puree, water and sugar in a saucepan. Stir until sugar is dissolved. Take off heat.

Squeeze the soft gelatine, releasing as much water as you can. Strain the liquid through a fine sieve into a bowl and let it cool.

Pour into a lamington tray or a tray about 25 cm (9¾ in) x 15 cm (6 in) lined with baking paper, making sure paper hangs over the sides, which will make it easier to remove. Refrigerate until set.

Remove jelly from tray by lifting the edges of the paper. Then cut the jelly into cubes and use as a garnish with Coconut Rice Mousse.

RHUBARB JELLY

Makes 150 ml (5 fl oz)

5 stalks of rhubarb
caster (superfine) sugar
    (amount of sugar
    depends on rhubarb
    weight—for every 100 g
    (3½ oz) of rhubarb, use 50
    g (1¾ oz) of sugar)
15 ml (½ fl oz) gin
1½ gelatine sheets

This purple jelly is a colourful complement to my coconut panna cotta. Garnish with threads of Rhubarb Candy (see recipe). ~ Nadine

Preheat the oven to 150°C (300°F). Line a small roasting tray with baking paper.

If your rhubarb is very fibrous, first strip off the outer membrane with a small knife.

Cut the stalks into 3 cm (1¼ in) lengths. Toss together the rhubarb, caster sugar and gin. Allow this to sit aside for 20 minutes. Doing this will prevent your rhubarb from going pulpy during baking and it will retain its shape once cooled.

Place entire rhubarb contents into the roasting tray. Cover with foil and bake for 20 minutes or until the rhubarb has just softened and cooked through. Remove from the oven and allow rhubarb to cool down in its juices. Strain the rhubarb, reserving the liquid—make sure you have 250 ml (1 cup) of liquid.

Soften 1½ sheets of gelatine in cold water. Place rhubarb liquid in a small saucepan and bring to a simmer over a medium heat. Remove from heat and add squeezed gelatine sheets.

Stir until the gelatine has dissolved, then strain through fine sieve. Refrigerate until set. The leftover rhubarb pulp can be used as a topping on ice cream, cake or pudding.

PASSIONFRUIT JELLY

Makes 350 ml (12 fl oz)

250 g (8½ oz) passionfruit
    pulp
25 g (¾ oz) caster (superfine)
    sugar
2 titanium gelatine sheets
100 ml (3¾ fl oz) water

Combine with summer fruits and top with a scoop of Spiced Ice Cream for a simple refreshing dessert. Or use to garnish Chocolate Pudding with Soft Pistachio Centre & Ginger Foam. ~ Nathan

Line a small loaf tin or plastic container with baking paper.

Place the passionfruit pulp and sugar into a saucepan and over a low heat bring to a simmer.

Meanwhile soak the gelatine in the water to soften. After simmering the passionfruit and sugar for 10 minutes, add the gelatine and water to the saucepan. Stir well to dissolve the gelatine and strain the mixture through a fine sieve to remove the passionfruit seeds.

Pour the jelly into the lined tin. Refrigerate until set and cut into desired sizes or shapes and return to the refrigerator until required.

COCONUT PANNA COTTA
with rhubarb jelly, turmeric sugar & rhubarb candy

Serves enough for 10 dariole moulds or glasses, as in photo

COCONUT PANNA COTTA

400 ml (14 fl oz) thickened cream
100 ml (3½ fl oz) water
200 ml (7 fl oz) sugar
3 sheets gelatine
600 ml (21 fl oz) coconut cream
1 quantity Rhubarb Jelly

TO SERVE

Turmeric Sugar (see recipe)
Rhubarb Candy (see recipe)

Stunning to the eye, a striking colour combination. Carry the colours through with a garnish of bright Turmeric Sugar and Rhubarb Candy. ~ Nadine

Coconut Panna Cotta

Whip cream lightly until it just holds. Set aside in refrigerator.

Bring water and sugar to boil, cook out until soft ball stage (see Glossary). Allow to slightly cool.

Soften gelatine in cold water, drain and dissolve in the warm syrup.

Mix syrup with coconut cream. Fold coconut mix into the whipped cream gently.

Pour the panna cotta mix into the dariole moulds. Allow the moulds to set for at least 2 hours in the refrigerator.

When the panna cotta is set, make the Rhubarb Jelly and when the jelly is cool, pour gently onto the panna cotta. Allow to set in the refrigerator.

To Serve

Garnish each mould with Turmeric Sugar and Rhubarb Candy.

MANGO PANNA COTTA with LYCHEE, ORANGE, PASSIONFRUIT SALAD,
lime syrup & honey wafer

Serves 6

LYCHEE, ORANGE, PASSIONFRUIT SALAD
12 lychees
2 oranges
2 passionfruit

LIME SYRUP
125 g (4 oz) caster
    (superfine) sugar
125 ml (4 fl oz) water
100 ml (3½ fl oz) lime juice
1 lime, zest only

MANGO PANNA COTTA
50 ml (1¾ oz) water
100 g (3½ oz) caster
    (superfine) sugar
1½ gelatine sheets
100 ml (2¾ fl oz) coconut
    cream
200 ml (7 fl oz) mango puree
200 ml (7 fl oz) cream

This dessert, with its fresh fruit and zingy flavours, will take you straight to the tropics. Perfumed passionfruit, luscious mango, creamy coconut and exotic lychee will have your senses floating away on holidays. ~ Libby

Lychee, Orange, Passionfruit Salad
Using a small knife, peel the lychees, cut them in half and remove the seeds.

Remove the peel and white pith off the orange with the knife. Then run the knife between the membranes of the orange towards the centre of the fruit and cut out the individual segments. Remove any seeds.

Halve the passionfruit and scoop out the pulp.

Toss the fruit together in a bowl and keep refrigerated until needed.

Lime Syrup
Place the sugar and water into a heavy-based saucepan and boil over a medium heat. Reduce syrup by half, add the lime juice and bring back to a boil. Remove from heat, add lime zest and cool. Cover and keep stored in your refrigerator.

Mango Panna Cotta
Bring the water and sugar to the boil, remove from heat. Soften the gelatine sheets in cold water, then squeeze out the excess water and add them to the warm sugar syrup. Cool to room temperature.

72

TO SERVE

6 Crisp Honey Wafers (see recipe)

Place the sugar syrup and coconut cream into a bowl and mix together. Stir through the mango puree and strain all into another bowl.

Whip the cream to soft peaks and carefully fold through the mango mix until fully incorporated.

Lightly spray six 125 ml (4 fl oz) dariole moulds with non-stick spray. Pour in the mango panna cotta mix and place in the refrigerator to set overnight.

To Serve

Remove the panna cottas from the refrigerator. Run a small knife, dipped into very hot water, around the inside of each mould and turn the panna cotta out into the centre of each serving plate.

Place an even amount of lychee, orange and passionfruit salad along the side of each panna cotta. Drizzle the lime syrup over the panna cotta. Lean a Crisp Honey Wafer up against the panna cotta.

PALM SUGAR & LEMONGRASS PANNA COTTA

Serves 8

2 large stalks of lemongrass
440 ml (14 fl oz) whipping
  cream
150 ml (5 fl oz) full-cream
  milk
75 g (2½ oz) palm sugar
45 g (1½ oz) caster
  (superfine) sugar
2 leaves gelatine

TO SERVE
1 stalk lemongrass
sprigs of micro mint leaves

This panna cotta is extremely easy to make and simple to jazz up for a dinner party, by serving with some fresh fruits, jellies or sorbet. You can put your own twist on this recipe by changing the lemongrass with any Asian aromatic or spice.
~ Nathan

Bruise the lemongrass by hitting repeatedly with the back of a knife, pestle or meat mallet. Place the lemongrass, cream and milk into a saucepan and warm over a low heat. Once warm, add both palm sugar and caster (superfine) sugar and stir until the sugar is dissolved. Bring mixture to a light simmer for 20 minutes. Remove mixture from heat, cover and let the flavours infuse for half an hour.

After 20 minutes, soak the gelatine in some cold water for 5 minutes to allow it to soften. Place the panna cotta mixture back onto the heat and return to a simmer. Squeeze out any excess water from the gelatine and add the gelatine to the mixture. Stir until dissolved and strain the mixture through a fine sieve. Pour the panna cotta mixture into eight dariole moulds or ramekins and refrigerate for four hours or until set.

To Serve
Run a small knife, dipped into very hot water, around the inside of each mould and turn the panna cotta out into the centre of each serving plate. Garnish simply with some very finely julienned rings of lemongrass and sprigs of micro mint leaves. If desired, add a scoop of Mint or Lychee Lime Sorbet (see recipe).

PASSIONFRUIT PANNA COTTA

Serves 8

200 g (7 oz) caster (superfine) sugar
600 ml (21 fl oz) whipping cream
200 ml (7 fl oz) full-cream milk
2 vanilla beans (split lengthways)
200 ml (7 fl oz) fresh passionfruit pulp (about 6–8 passionfruit)
2 gelatine sheets

You can swap the passionfruit to any other fruit puree or pulp. Avoid sour, acidic fruits as they may curdle the mixture. Mango, custard apple, durian, guava or even cherries would be great. Just follow one simple rule: don't change the amount of cream! The milk and fruit pulp ratio can be altered according to taste, but needs to measure a total of 400 ml (14 fl oz). ~ Nathan

Place the sugar, cream, milk, vanilla and passionfruit into a saucepan and gently warm. Remove from the heat just before it boils.

Soak the gelatine in some cold water to soften for five minutes, place the panna cotta mixture back onto the heat (don't boil). Remove the gelatine from the water and squeeze out any excess water. Add the gelatine to the panna cotta mixture and stir until dissolved. Strain mixture through a fine sieve and pour into dariole moulds or ramekins. Refrigerate for a minimum of four hours or overnight until set.

To Serve
Run a small knife, dipped into very hot water, around the inside of each mould and turn the panna cotta out into the centre of each serving plate. Serve with a squeeze of passionfruit juice or slices of tropical fruit like mango or papaya. If desired, add a scoop of Lychee Lime Sorbet (see recipe).

BANANA BAVAROIS, SALTED PEANUT
caramel, chocolate rum sauce &
dark chocolate curls

Don't let the length of this recipe scare you off trying it. The chocolate sauce, curls and salted peanut caramel can all be made days ahead of the bavarois. This is a popular dessert at the Spirit House, so I'm sure your efforts will be well received.
~ Libby

Serves 10

CHOCOLATE CURLS

1 quantity Chocolate Curls
(see recipe in Bling
section)

CHOCOLATE RUM SAUCE

40 g (1½ oz) corn syrup
20 ml (²/3 fl oz) vegetable oil
10 g (1/3 oz) caster
(superfine) sugar
110 ml (3½ fl oz) cream
150 g (5 oz) dark chocolate,
chopped
20 ml (²/3 fl oz) milk
30 ml (1 fl oz) dark rum

SALTED PEANUT CARAMEL

1 quantity Salted Peanut
Caramel (see recipe in
Bling section)

COCONUT CAKE BASE

160 g (5½ oz) unsalted
butter, soft

Chocolate Curls
Can be made up to 7 days ahead of time.

Chocolate and Rum Sauce
In a saucepan, bring the the corn syrup, oil, sugar and 55 ml (1¾ fl oz) of cream to a simmer over a medium heat.

Place the chocolate into a bowl and pour over the warm cream mixture. Whisk in the milk, rum and the remaining 55 ml (1¾ fl oz) of cream until combined. Strain and cool. Keep stored in an airtight container in the refrigerator for up to 1 month.

Salted Peanut Caramel
Can be made up to 7 days ahead of time.

Coconut Cake Base
Preheat the oven to 170°C (340°F) and line an 18 cm (7 in) × 28 cm (11 in) oven tray with baking paper. Line six 6½ cm (2½ in) tall, 5cm (2 in) wide cylindrical moulds with baking paper and set aside.

Cream butter and sugar. Add one egg and mix well.

Combine the flours with the desiccated coconut and add to the butter mix. Add the last egg and once it is well combined, spread the mixture out onto your lined oven tray. Bake for 20 minutes, or until golden and cooked through. Remove from the oven and cool. Using lined cylindrical moulds as cutters, press each mould firmly down into the cake and twist to remove the cake rounds. Place the moulds

150 g (5 oz) caster (superfine) sugar

2 eggs

20 g (²/₃ oz) tapioca flour

20 g (²/₃ oz) cornflour (cornstarch)

160 g (5½ oz) desiccated coconut

BANANA BAVAROIS

165 ml (5½ fl oz) milk

165 ml (5½ fl oz) cream

3 ripe bananas, chopped

½ vanilla bean, split lengthways

65 g (2 oz) caster (superfine) sugar

4 egg yolks

165 ml (5½ fl oz) cream

2 sheets titanium gelatine (see Glossary)

TO SERVE

10 g (¹/₃ oz) salted peanuts, finely chopped for garnishing

pinch sea salt, for garnishing

with their fitted bases into the refrigerator. Keep any leftover coconut cake stored in an airtight container in the refrigerator for up to 5 days.

Banana Bavarois

Combine the milk, 165 ml (5½ fl oz) cream, bananas, vanilla bean and one tablespoon of the sugar into a saucepan. Place over a medium heat and bring to a simmer. Remove from heat and set aside for 20 minutes so the flavours infuse.

Return the saucepan to the heat and bring back to a simmer. Take off the heat, strain and discard the solids.

In a bowl, whisk together the egg yolks and remaining sugar. Slowly whisk in the warm banana cream mix.

Place the bowl over a saucepan of simmering water; make sure the water level is well below the base of the bowl. Stir the egg mixture constantly and gently with a wooden spoon until it begins to thicken and you can draw a line with your finger along the back of your wooden spoon. Remove from the heat.

Soften the gelatine sheets in cold water. Squeeze out any excess water, stir into the warm custard and, once dissolved, strain custard into a clean bowl. Place bowl inside a larger bowl filled with iced water and stir until cooled to room temperature.

Whip the remaining 165 ml (5½ fl oz) of cream to soft peaks. Fold through the banana custard.

Remove lined moulds from the refrigerator and give their insides a light spray with non-stick spray. Pour bavarois mix into each mould, straight over the top of the coconut cake base, filling to the top of the mould. Transfer the bavarois to the refrigerator and allow them to set overnight.

To Serve

Take the bavarois out of the refrigerator and push them out of their moulds. Place each bavarois in the centre of serving plates. Top each one with a Chocolate Curl and large tablespoon of Salted Peanut Caramel, allowing it to run down the sides. Dot some sauce around the plate and sprinkle with the finely chopped peanuts and sea salt flakes.

PINEAPPLE CHILLI SOUP

Serves 6

PINEAPPLE SOUP
1 large ripe pineapple
50 g (1½ oz) caster
    (superfine) sugar
pineapple juice to taste
75 ml (2½ fl oz) Champagne
    or sparkling wine

SUGAR SYRUP
250 g (8 oz) caster
    (superfine) sugar
500 ml (17 fl oz) water

OPTIONAL CHILLI SYRUP
50 ml (1¾ fl oz) sugar syrup
pinch chilli flakes

Easy to prepare, tastes great—an excellent way to start a cocktail or dinner party. Omit the chilli if you prefer or add your own little twist such as Ginger Foam. You could also use the base Ginger Foam recipe and add your own twist to the foam such as lemon, lime or passionfruit. ~ Nathan

Pineapple Soup
Cut off the pineapple base and top, stand the fruit upright on a board and slice away the skin following the natural curve of the fruit. Cut pineapple into quarters lengthways and remove the tough core. Roughly chop the pineapple flesh into pieces and toss chunks with the sugar.

Place a large heavy-based frying pan on a high heat, add the pineapple and toss for a few minutes until the pineapple begins to soften and slightly caramelise. Place pineapple into a food processor or blender and process to fine puree. Pass the puree through a fine strainer into a bowl, extracting as much juice as possible. Dispose of the pulp. Taste the juice and balance with pineapple juice, Champagne and a little more sugar if needed. Cover bowl with cling film and chill until required.

Sugar Syrup
Place the sugar and water into a saucepan and dissolve the sugar over low heat When sugar is dissolved, bring the syrup up to a simmer and boil for 5 minutes. Allow to cool, then place the syrup into a squeeze bottle or airtight container. This syrup will last in the refrigerator for a couple of weeks.

Optional Chilli Syrup

Place the sugar syrup and chilli flakes into a saucepan and slowly bring to a simmer over a low heat. Take off heat and let steep for 10 minutes, then strain through a fine strainer.

To Serve

Place the pineapple soup into serving glass, like a champagne flute, or small tea cups. Drizzle the chilli sugar syrup down the inside of the glass. If you so choose, top with a flavoured foam (see Chocolate Pudding with Soft Pistachio Centre, Passionfruit Jelly & Ginger Foam) then garnish with a sprig of mint, some Candied Chilli or a chilli flower or fresh piece of pineapple.

COCONUT & LIME POSSET
with sugared lime segments

Serves 6

200 ml (7 fl oz) lime juice
250 g (8 oz) caster (superfine) sugar
500 ml (18 fl oz) Kara UHT coconut cream (see Glossary)
2 sheets gelatine
2 limes, finely segmented and rolled in sugar for the garnish

This tasty little number will keep you coming back and making it for years to come. Its smooth silky texture will leave your guests trying to guess how you made it. ~ Nathan

Strain the lime juice through a fine sieve. Place the juice in a saucepan with the sugar and bring to the boil over a low heat, stirring continuously until the sugar is completely dissolved. Leave this in a warm spot, like the back of the stove.

Meanwhile, soften the gelatine in some cold water for about 5 minutes. In a heavy-based pan, bring the coconut cream to a boil, then pour it over the warm lime and sugar mixture. Squeeze out excess water in gelatine and add to mixture. Stir all mixtures together and then strain into a jug through a fine sieve. Pour into your desired serving bowl and set in the refrigerator for at least 2 hours or until set.

To Serve
Arrange bowls on serving plates and garnish with sugar-coated lime segments and some finely julienned fresh young coconut.

TIP
Make sure that you use Kara brand coconut cream for this, as most other brands will just be too thin. You should be able to find it in any Asian grocer. If you can't find it simply use double cream and feel free to change the lime juice to lemon juice. Make sure you only use freshly squeezed juice.

FIRE

CHOCOLATE PUDDING

with soft pistachio centre, passionfruit jelly &
ginger foam

Serves 10

PUDDING BATTER

250 g (8½ oz) dark chocolate
250 g (8½ oz) unsalted butter
200 g (6½ oz) plain (all-
    purpose) flour
185 g (6o.oz) caster
    (superfine) sugar
1 teaspoon baking powder
8 large eggs

PISTACHIO CENTRE

100 g (3½ oz) white chocolate
75 ml (2½ fl oz) cream
30 g (1 oz) pistachio paste
    (Make pistachio paste,
    by blanching a handful
    of pistachio nuts in some
    boiling water for around
    5 minutes, then drain and
    blend)

At Spirit House, we serve this pudding with
passionfruit jelly and ginger foam. It walks, or rather,
runs out the door. You can prepare this well in advance
as all the components can be made separately and
refrigerated for around five days. Use other nuts too,
like cashews, macadamias or Brazil for this recipe. ~
Nathan

Pudding Batter

Bring a saucepan half-full of water to the boil, then
reduce to a simmer. Chop the chocolate and butter
into pieces and place them into a large heatproof
bowl. Place the bowl on top of the saucepan. Stir the
chocolate and butter every few minutes until smooth
and completely melted; remove from the heat.

  Meanwhile, sift the flour, sugar and baking powder
into a large bowl. Make a well in the centre, break in the
eggs and whisk to a paste. Pour this over the melted
chocolate mixture and whisk until smooth. If you find
any lumps, pass the mixture through a fine sieve. Place
the mixture into an airtight container until required.

Pistachio Centre

Bring a saucepan half-full of water to the boil, then
reduce to a simmer. Chop the white chocolate and
place into a heatproof bowl, add the cream and
pistachio paste to bowl and place over the simmering
saucepan. Stir the mixture every couple of minutes until
the chocolate is completely melted and the mixture is
smooth.

LIGHT GINGER FOAM

75 g (2½ oz) double cream
175 ml (6 fl oz) full-cream
    milk
35 g (1 oz) caster (superfine)
    sugar
15 g (½ oz) fresh ginger,
    peeled and grated
¾ leaf gelatine sheet

TO SERVE

1 quantity Passionfruit Jelly
    (see recipe)

Leave the mixture to cool, then place into an airtight container and refrigerate until required.

Light Ginger Foam

Place the double cream, milk, sugar and ginger into a small saucepan over a low heat until it reaches a simmer. Once simmering, take off heat and leave in a warm spot to infuse for 10–15 minutes.

Soak the gelatine in cold water to soften for about 5 minutes. Return the cream mixture to the heat and again, bring to a simmer then take off heat. Remove the gelatine from the water, squeeze out any excess water and stir the gelatine into the cream mixture until dissolved. Strain the contents through a fine sieve to remove the grated ginger.

Chill the mixture for a couple of hours until partially set. With an electric beater, whisk the mixture for about 5 minutes until light and foamy and return to the refrigerator until required. Just before serving, whisk it again until thick and creamy, then place into a piping bag and serve as desired.

To Serve

Preheat an oven to 220°C (430°F). Grease 10 metal rings or pudding ramekins, about 5 cm (2 in) in diameter, with softened butter. When the oven is hot, spoon or pipe the pudding batter into the moulds until half full. Add a teaspoon of pistachio mixture into the middle of each pudding, and then cover with more pudding mixture to enclose the pistachio mix. Bake for ten minutes. Remove from the oven and allow to cool for a couple of minutes—this makes them easier to get out of the moulds. If they are still a little stuck use the point of a small paring knife to help them out. Serve immediately with the Ginger Foam and garnish with Passionfruit Jelly.

SWEET POTATO & GINGER PUDDING
with malibu poached pears

Serves 6

SWEET POTATO & GINGER PUDDING

300 g (1½ oz) sweet potato, peeled

250 ml (8½ fl oz) coconut cream

60 g (2 oz) brown sugar

2 eggs lightly beaten

10 g (1/3 oz) fresh grated ginger

10 g (1/3 oz) fresh grated nutmeg

200 ml (7 fl oz) dollop cream to serve

MALIBU PEARS

2 pears

750 ml (24 fl oz) water

220 g (8 oz) caster (superfine) sugar

1 vanilla bean

100 ml (2¾ fl oz) Malibu (rum liqueur)

My mum is a nurse and very health conscious, so she rarely eats desserts—but for this pudding, she always makes an exception. ~ Renee

Sweet Potato & Ginger Pudding

Preheat the oven to 180°C (350°F). Shave 12–15 thin strips off the sweet potato and set aside for garnish.

Steam rest of sweet potato until soft, lightly mash and set aside to cool slightly.

In a mixer with a paddle attachment, put sweet potato, coconut cream, brown sugar, eggs, ginger and nutmeg, blend until smooth.

Pour mix into six ramekins 9 cm (3½ in) in diameter and bake for 20 minutes or until firm to touch. Allow to cool slightly then refrigerate until needed.

These puddings can be served warm or cold. To reheat return to oven for 5–10 minutes.

Malibu Pears

Peel and quarter pears, remove seeds and core.

Place water, sugar and split vanilla bean in saucepan, over medium heat dissolve sugar and simmer for 5 minutes. Add Malibu and pears.

TO SERVE

slices of Candied Sweet
Potato (see recipe)

Cut some greaseproof paper into a circle and place on the surface of poaching liquid, this will help keep pears from rising above water level and poaching unevenly.

Simmer pears for 15–20 minutes or until tender. Cooking time may vary depending on ripeness. Pears can be served warm or cold. Store in poaching liquid in refrigerator until needed.

To Serve
Warm pudding in ramekin, thinly slice pear quarter and curl on top of pudding with a little of the pear syrup.

Using a warm spoon, scoop some dollop cream on top of the pear or serve in a small side dish or on a Chinese spoon.

Garnish with some slices of Candied Sweet Potato.

STEAMED GINGER PUDDING
with pickled cumquats

Serves 6

PICKLED CUMQUATS

1 kg (2 lb 4 oz) cumquats
1 kg (2 lb 4 oz) caster
 (superfine) sugar
500 ml (17½ fl oz) rice
 vinegar
500 ml (17½ fl oz) water
2 cinnamon quills
5 cloves
2 star anise
1 teaspoon (5 g) black
 pepper
1 teaspoon (5 g) szechwan
 pepper

GINGER PUDDING

150 g (5 oz) candied ginger
40 g (1½ oz) golden syrup
20 ml (2/3 fl oz) ginger wine
20 g (2/3 oz) glucose syrup
2 eggs, separated
40 g (1½ oz) sugar
10 g (1/3 oz) butter, melted
100 ml (2¾ fl oz) milk
150 g (5 oz) self-raising (self-
 rising) flour

When cumquats are in season, pickle them in sterilised jars and store in the pantry. Packed with Vitamin C, cumquats are a wonderful accompaniment to braised poultry dishes, winter puddings, summer desserts—and anything containing chocolate! ~ Libby

Pickled Cumquats

Put cumquats in a large saucepan and cover with water. Bring to the boil, reduce to a simmer and cook for 25 minutes, uncovered. Strain and set aside.

Bring remaining ingredients to a boil in a large pot, add cumquats and simmer for 1 hour. Transfer cumquats to clean jars, pour pickling liquid over cumquats and seal while hot. Store for two weeks before using. Once open, keep refrigerated.

Ginger Pudding

Preheat the oven to 180°C (350°F).

Blend ginger, golden syrup, ginger wine and glucose together and set aside.

Whisk egg yolks and sugar until pale. Add butter, then add ginger mix. Fold in the milk and flour to the mixture. Whisk egg whites to a stiff peak and fold into the mix.

Spoon six 125 ml (4 fl oz) buttered moulds three-quarters full of pudding mix, and bake in a water bath in the oven for 30 minutes. Stand in moulds for a little while before turning out onto a serving plate. Spoon a few pickled cumquats onto each pudding, drizzle with a little of the pickling liquid. Serve with whipped cream, Spiced or Cinnamon Ice Cream (see recipe).

STEAMED BANANA PISTACHIO PUDDING
with cardamom toffee sauce

Serves 6

PISTACHIO TOPPING

50 g (1¾ oz) butter, softened
50 g (1¾ oz) dark palm sugar
25 g (¾ oz) pistachios,
    chopped

STEAMED BANANA PISTACHIO
    PUDDING

1 large ripe banana
1 lemon
125 g (4 oz) butter, softened
125 g (4 oz) caster
    (superfine) sugar
3 medium eggs
100 g (3½ oz) self-raising
    (self-rising) flour
¼ teaspoon salt
½ teaspoon baking powder
25 g (¾ oz) pistachios,
    chopped
75 g (2½ oz) almond meal

Warm pudding, delicious toffee sauce and Anglaise—the ultimate comfort food. Serves six, but I recommend making a double batch as it won't last long. ~ Nadine

Pistachio Topping
Lightly grease individual pudding moulds or a pudding basin.
    Cream butter and sugar, spread over base of moulds and sprinkle with chopped nuts.

Steamed Banana Pistachio Pudding
Preheat oven to 180°C (350°F).
    Mash banana and grate the zest and squeeze the juice of the lemon.
    Place the butter, sugar, eggs, flour, salt, baking powder, lemon juice and zest in a food processor. Mix or whizz until smooth and creamy. Add chopped nuts, almond meal and banana, whizz until combined. Spoon into pudding moulds, cover each mould with foil greased with butter. Place the moulds into a heatproof dish, pour enough water into the dish to come halfway up the side of the moulds.
    Steam for 1 hour for individual puddings, 2 hours for a large pudding. Check with a skewer to see if it is cooked; if it comes out clean, they are ready.

CARDAMOM TOFFEE SAUCE

300 ml (10½ fl oz) double
  cream
170 g (5½ oz) dark palm
  sugar
3 cardamom pods, crushed
1 vanilla bean, scraped
60 ml (2 fl oz) glucose syrup
70 g (2½ oz) unsalted butter

TO SERVE

Anglaise Ice Cream Base
  (see recipe)
1–2 bananas, thinly sliced or
  some Candied Banana
  Slices (see recipe), for
  garnish

Cardamom Toffee Sauce

Put 150 ml (5 fl oz) cream in a saucepan, add sugar, cardamom, vanilla bean, glucose and butter, slowly bring to the boil. When sugar is dissolved, continue boiling for about 10 minutes until it becomes a toffee colour, stirring all the time so that it doesn't burn.

Remove from the heat and cool. When cold, stir in remaining cream, remove cardamom pods and vanilla bean. Serve at room temperature with Anglaise Ice Cream Base (see recipe).

To Serve

Un-mould puddings, place on plate, pour over Cardamom Toffee Sauce, and Anglaise Base, whipped cream or ice cream.

Add a garnish of thinly sliced fresh banana, or for extra crunch, some Candied Banana Slices.

DARK CHOCOLATE & STAR ANISE RICE PUDDING

with caramelised banana, coconut cream & crunchy candied coconut

Serves 6

DARK CHOCOLATE & STAR ANISE RICE PUDDING

225 g (½ lb) white rice, medium grain
240 g (8¾ oz) caster (superfine) sugar
90 g (3 oz) cocoa powder
2.25 litres (4¾ pt) milk
6 star anise
120 g (¼ lb) dark chocolate, chopped

WHIPPED COCONUT CREAM

125 ml (4 fl oz) coconut cream
15 g (½ oz) icing (confectioners') sugar, sifted
pinch salt

CARAMELISED BANANAS

2 bananas, ripe and firm
60 g (2 oz) brown sugar
30 g (1 oz) butter

I love dark chocolate. For me, the richer it is, the better it is. This recipe is definitely for chocolate lovers like myself. However, should you prefer, simply reduce the amount of chocolate stirred through at the end. ~ Libby

Dark Chocolate and Star Anise Rice Pudding
Run the rice under cold water until the water runs clear.

Place the sugar, cocoa powder, milk and star anise into a saucepan and place over a medium heat, whisking to combine. Allow the mixture to come to the boil.

Add the washed rice and bring it back to a boil. Turn the heat down to its lowest setting and cook, uncovered, for 30 minutes, or until the rice is cooked through, stirring occasionally.

When rice is cooked, remove the pot from heat and scoop out the star anise. Stir through the chocolate until it is completely melted.

Whipped Coconut Cream
Whisk the coconut cream with the sugar and salt until soft peaks form. Cover and refrigerate until needed.

Caramelised Bananas
Slice the bananas, on an angle, into 7 mm (¼ in) thick pieces. Roll them into the brown sugar and press down to coat well. Heat a large frypan over medium heat. Add the butter and when it begins to bubble, add

TO SERVE
Crunchy Candied Coconut
(see recipe)

the banana pieces. Allow to cook for 1–2 minutes each side, or until lovely and caramelised. Remove from heat and serve while still warm.

To Serve

When your rice is in its final stages of cooking, prepare and cook your bananas. Divide the warm rice pudding into six individual 125 ml (4 fl oz) serving bowls or glasses. Top with a dollop of Whipped Coconut Cream and the warm Caramelised Bananas. Sprinkle the Crunchy Candied Coconut across the top of the puddings.

GINGER COCONUT TAPIOCA PUDDINGS,
roasted pineapple & candied ginger chips

Serves 6

ROASTED PINEAPPLE
½ pineapple
45 g (1½ oz) brown sugar
60 ml (2 fl oz) orange juice
20 g (²/3 oz) honey

GINGER COCONUT TAPIOCA PUDDINGS
140 g (5 oz) tapioca, small pearl
330 ml (11 fl oz) milk
500 ml (16 fl oz) coconut cream
160 g (5½ oz) caster (superfine) sugar
1 vanilla bean, split lengthways
1 egg yolk
45 g (1½ oz) stem ginger, minced

TO SERVE
1 quantity Candied Ginger Chips (see recipe)

Here tapioca pearls make up a wonderfully creamy gluten-free dessert. The chewy little pearls are a lovely contrast to the smooth coconut and the natural sweetness of the roasted pineapple. ~ Libby

Roasted Pineapple
Preheat the oven to 220°C (420°F). Line a tray with baking paper.

Peel and core the pineapple and cut into 2 cm (¾ in) pieces.

In a bowl, whisk together the sugar, orange juice and honey. Add pineapple pieces and toss to coat. Spread the pineapple over the tray and roast in the oven for 30 minutes, or until tender and caramelised. Remove from the oven, drizzle over any remaining sugar mixture and allow to cool. Store in an airtight container in the refrigerator for 3 days.

Ginger Coconut Tapioca Puddings
Soak the tapioca pearls in cold water for 20 minutes, strain and discard water.

In a large saucepan, whisk the milk, coconut cream, sugar, vanilla bean and tapioca over a very low heat until tapioca is translucent. Whisk in the yolk. When the mixture reaches 71°C (160°F) on a sugar thermometer, remove from heat and cover the surface of the tapioca with cling film. Set aside at room temperature for 40 minutes. Remove the cling film and vanilla bean and stir in the ginger.

To Serve
Portion the tapioca pudding into six 125 ml (4 fl oz) serving bowls. Top with some warm Roasted Pineapple and sprinkle over with Candied Ginger Chips.

PUMPKIN CRÈME CARAMEL
with coconut & roasted rice crunch

Serves 6

COCONUT & ROASTED RICE CRUNCH
25 g (¾ oz) jasmine rice
60 g (2 oz) desiccated coconut
30 g (1 oz) caster (superfine) sugar
1 egg white

CARAMEL
200 g (7 oz) caster (superfine) sugar
100 ml (3½ oz) cold water
40 ml (1½ fl oz) hot water

This crème caramel has a lovely smooth texture. Adding the crunchy coconut and roasted rice brings a whole other texture to the plate. I believe even the staunchest pumpkin-hater would enjoy this sweet, creamy caramel dessert. ~ Libby

Coconut & Roasted Rice Crunch
Preheat the oven to 180°C (350°F).

Place the rice onto a tray and bake for 20 minutes or until golden. Allow rice to cool, then give it a quick pound in a mortar and pestle to slightly break it up.

Combine all ingredients together in a bowl and spread out onto a lined baking tray. Return to the oven for another 20 minutes, stirring regularly until golden and crunchy.

Remove from oven and allow to cool on the tray. Keep stored in an airtight container, away from any moisture, for one week.

Caramel
Place sugar and cold water into a heavy-based saucepan, over a medium heat and allow to boil. Once boiling, it will slowly start to colour and turn golden. As soon as the syrup begins to smoke, remove from heat and add hot water.

Be careful, as the boiling caramel will bubble up and spit. Swirl pan until water is all combined. Divide this caramel between six 125 ml (4 fl oz) dariole moulds.

PUMPKIN CRÈME

1 medium pumpkin to make
    125 ml (4 fl oz) pumpkin
    puree
50 ml (1¾ fl oz) water
100 g (3½ oz) caster
    (superfine) sugar
2 titanium gelatine sheets
    (see Glossary)
180 ml (6 fl oz) coconut cream
pinch ground cinnamon
pinch ground star anise
200 ml (7 oz) cream

Pumpkin Crème

Preheat oven to 200°C (400°F).

Skin and deseed the pumpkin and dice into 2 cm (¾ in) pieces. Bake, covered, for 30 minutes, or until well cooked. Puree cooked pumpkin, push it through a fine sieve and allow to cool. Measure out 125 ml (4 fl oz) of puree for this recipe.

Bring water and sugar to the boil and remove from heat. Soften gelatine sheets in cold water, squeeze out excess water and add them to the warm sugar syrup. Cool syrup to room temperature.

In a bowl, mix together the sugar syrup and coconut cream. Strain mix, then stir through the pumpkin puree. Add in the cinnamon and star anise.

Whip cream to soft peaks and carefully fold through pumpkin mix until fully incorporated.

Lightly spray the dariole moulds with non-stick spray. Pour in the pumpkin crème mix, on top of the caramel. Place into the refrigerator to set overnight.

To Serve

Dip the dariole mould tops into hot water for a few seconds to dissolve the caramel. Run a small knife, dipped into hot water, around the inside of each mould and turn out onto desired serving plate. Scatter the Roasted Rice and Coconut Crunch across the top of each crème caramel.

RHUBARB, APPLE & GINGER CRUMBLE
with puffed rice & cinnamon ice cream

Serves 6

STEWED APPLES

500 g (17½ oz) green apples
15 g (½ oz) caster (superfine)
    sugar
10 ml (1/3 fl oz) water
1 squeeze lemon

BAKED RHUBARB

5 stalks of rhubarb
15 ml (½ fl oz) gin
caster (superfine) sugar
    (amount depends on
    rhubarb weight—for
    every 100 g (3½ oz) of
    rhubarb, use 50 g (1¾
    oz) of caster (superfine)
    sugar)

This crumble top is gluten-free. Enjoy the delicious sensory experience as you scoop through the golden crisp top into the steaming fruit below. For a special treat, serve with Cinnamon Ice Cream. ~ Libby

Stewed Apples
Peel and dice apples into 2 cm (¾ in) pieces.

Put all the ingredients into a small saucepan, over a medium heat and cover with lid.

Once the apple is steaming, remove lid and stir occasionally for the next 5 minutes. The apples are cooked when they have softened, yet still retain their shape and slight bite.

Remove from heat and allow to cool down to room temperature. Keep stored in an airtight container in the refrigerator for up to 3 days.

Baked Rhubarb
Preheat the oven to 150°C (300°F). Line a small roasting tray with baking paper.

If your rhubarb is very fibrous, first strip off the outer membrane with a small knife.

Cut the stalks into 3 cm (1¼ in) lengths. Toss the rhubarb, sugar and gin together and set aside for 20 minutes. This will prevent your rhubarb from turning pulpy during baking and it will retain its shape once cooled.

PUFFED RICE CRUMBLE

60 g (2 oz) butter, diced
60 g (2 oz) raw sugar
40 g (1½ oz) almond meal
20 g (²/3 oz) puffed rice

TO SERVE

30 g (1oz) stem ginger,
    chopped
1 quantity Cinnamon Ice
    Cream (see recipe)
Sugar Garnish (see recipe)

Place entire rhubarb contents into the roasting tray, cover with foil and bake for 20 minutes in the oven, or until the rhubarb has just softened and cooked through. Remove from the oven and allow rhubarb to cool down in its juices.

Once cool, pack into an airtight container and keep stored in the refrigerator for up to three days.

Puffed Rice Crumble
Rub the butter and raw sugar together until the mixture resembles breadcrumbs. Rub in the almond meal and then fold though the puffed rice.

Keep in an airtight container in the refrigerator for up to one week.

To Serve
Place apple pieces into the base of the six individual 125ml (4 oz) ovenproof serving dishes. Add a layer of rhubarb and scatter over the chopped stem ginger. Cover the lot with a full layer of crumble mix. Place crumbles onto the top shelf of a preheated 180°C (350°F) oven for 15 minutes, or until they are warmed through and begin to bubble at the top edges.

Remove crumbles from oven and place into the centre of six individual serving plates. Top each crumble with a scoop of Cinnamon Ice Cream, and a Sugar Garnish for a decorative finish.

CARAMELISED BANANA CAKE, PASSIONFRUIT LEMONGRASS SYRUP
& coconut rum ice cream

Serves 6

CARAMELISED BANANA CAKE
20 g (²/₃ oz) butter
160 g (5½ oz) brown sugar
60 ml (2 fl oz) water
8 small bananas (sliced)
4 eggs
220 g (7 oz) caster (superfine)
　　sugar
1 vanilla bean, split
　　lengthwise, scraped
150 g (5 oz) plain (all-
　　purpose) flour
1 teaspoon baking powder
150 g (5 oz) butter, melted
85 g (3 oz) desiccated
　　coconut

PASSIONFRUIT LEMONGRASS
SYRUP
4 passionfruit
1 lemongrass stalk, outer
　　husks removed, halved
60 ml (2 fl oz) water
30 g (1 oz) caster (superfine)
　　sugar

TO SERVE
Coconut Rum Ice Cream (see
　　recipe)

*This simple but yummy cake is a summer delight
and can be served with or without the ice cream.
~ Nadine*

Caramelised Banana Cake
Preheat oven to 160°C (325°F).

Place butter, sugar and water in a pan over low heat and stir until sugar has dissolved. Bring to the boil, cook for 3–4 minutes until mixture thickens. Pour into a 22 cm (9 in) square cake tin lined with baking paper.

Place banana slices on top of the caramel.

Place eggs, sugar and scraped vanilla bean in electric mixer, beat until pale and fluffy. Fold in sifted flour and baking powder. Add the extra butter and desiccated coconut, fold in well. Pour mix over banana caramel and bake for 45–50 minutes.

Test with a skewer or paring knife. Allow to come to room temperature before serving.

Passionfruit Lemongrass Syrup
Remove pulp from passionfruit and place pulp, lemongrass, water and sugar in saucepan. Stir over medium heat until sugar is dissolved.

Bring to the boil, cook for 2–3 minutes until slightly thickened. Take off heat and remove lemongrass stalks.

To Serve
Turn out cake upside down so that the caramelised banana is on top. Cut into desired size with a hot, wet knife. Drizzle cake slices with syrup and add a scoop of Coconut Rum Ice Cream on the side.

118

ORANGE CAKE

with citrus syrup & spiced ice cream

Serves 6

ORANGE CAKE

1 orange
85 g (3 oz) caster (superfine)
   sugar
2 eggs
15 g (½ oz) butter, softened
85 g (3 oz) almond meal
½ teaspoon baking powder

When the kids' weekend sports are over, I'm left with half a bag of oranges so I spoil the family with these sweet and tangy, gluten-free, orange cakes. If you are entertaining, dress the cakes up with Citrus Syrup and Spiced Ice Cream.
~ Renee

Orange Cake

Preheat the oven to 180°C (350°F). Grease 6 muffin tins with 9 cm (3½ in) diameter, line bases with greaseproof paper.

Wash orange, place in a saucepan and cover with water, boil for 1 hour. Keep an eye on the water level; you may need to add more water. Remove orange from water and allow to cool slightly, the orange should be soft. Roughly chop orange removing any pips. Blend orange in food processor and set aside.

With an electric mixer whisk sugar and eggs until light and fluffy. Add softened butter and mix through.

Add almond meal, baking powder and orange—mix until well combined.

Pour into muffin tray and bake for 45 minutes or until golden brown on top and springs back when touched.

Allow to cool, run a knife around edges of cake, turn out onto a cooling rack to cool completely.

CITRUS SYRUP

75g (2½ oz) sugar
100 ml (2¾ fl oz) water
1 vanilla bean
150 ml (5 fl oz) fresh orange
    juice strained
1 orange, zest and
    segmented
½ teaspoon lemon zest and
    juice
½ teaspoon lime zest and
    juice

TO SERVE

1 quantity Spiced Ice Cream
    (see recipe)
1 orange, segmented

Citrus Syrup

Place sugar, water, vanilla and 100 ml (2¾ fl oz) of orange juice in a saucepan and reduce by one-third.

Add 50 ml (2 fl oz) orange juice, all the lemon juice and zest, lime juice and zest, plus orange zest. Reduce to a syrup consistency.

Segment one orange. Remove all peel and pith, slice on either side of membrane to the middle of orange continuing all the way round so you are left with crescent shape orange pieces.

When syrup is reduced remove from heat. Add orange segments, let cool, then place in refrigerator until needed

To Serve

Place each orange cake on a dessert plate, top with a scoop of Spiced Ice Cream drizzled with citrus syrup and orange segments.

FLOURLESS CHOCOLATE CAKE
with chocolate chilli mousse & raspberry champagne jelly

Serves 8–10

FLOURLESS CHOCOLATE CAKE

200 g (7 oz) dark chocolate

150 g (5 oz) unsalted butter

5 eggs, separated

120 g (4 oz) caster (superfine) sugar

30 g (1 oz) cocoa powder

1 teaspoon icing (confectioners') sugar

TO SERVE

1 quantity Chocolate Chilli Mousse (see recipe)

1 quantity Raspberry Champagne Jelly (see recipe)

One of my family's favourites. If, like me, you're always pushed for time, just cook this beautifully moist, gluten-free cake and serve with whipped cream or ice cream. When you really want to impress, serve with Chocolate Chilli Mousse and Raspberry Champagne Jelly. ~ Renee

Flourless Chocolate Cake

Grease 15 x 25 cm (6 x 10 in) cake tin and line with baking paper.

Melt chocolate and butter over double boiler without stirring, making sure the water doesn't touch the bottom of the bowl.

Whip sugar and egg yolks until light and fluffy. Add cooled chocolate butter to yolk mix. When combined, add the sifted cocoa powder.

Whip egg white to soft peaks and then fold into mix, one-third at a time. Pour mix into cake tin and chill for 30 minutes before baking.

Bake cake for 30 minute intervals: first at 175°C (330°F) then 160°C (325°F) and finally 150°C (300°F). Allow to cool slightly before removing from tin. Cake will drop on cooling.

Refrigerate cake before portioning. Run a knife under hot water to get a clean cut, trim up sides and cut cake into six portions. Refrigerate until 15 minutes before serving.

To Serve

Bring cake to room temperature, place on serving dish. Cut into slices and, using a warm spoon, add a scoop of Chocolate Chilli Mousse on top of each slice, then scatter diced Raspberry Champagne Jellies around the side. Lightly dust the cake with the icing sugar.

fire

123

WARM GINGER CHOCOLATE SOUFFLÉ
with palm sugar & tamarind ice cream

Serves 6

GINGER CHOCOLATE GANACHE
125 g (4 oz) dark chocolate,
roughly chopped
125 ml (4 fl oz) cream
30 g (1 oz) fresh ginger,
peeled and sliced

GINGER PASTRY CREAM
1 vanilla bean, split and
seeds scraped
600 ml (20 fl oz) milk
60 g (2 oz) ginger, peeled
and sliced
120 g (4 oz) caster
(superfine) sugar
6 egg yolks
30 g (1 oz) cornflour
(cornstarch)
30 g (1 oz) plain (all-purpose)
flour

Soufflés don't deserve their difficult reputation. This recipe is not hard—it's simply a flavoured pastry cream combined with a French meringue to produce a lovely light, moist soufflé. Voilà—sour/ sweet tamarind meets hot fragrant ginger. ~ Libby

Ginger Chocolate Ganache
Melt chocolate over a saucepan of simmering water.
   In another saucepan, bring the cream and ginger to a simmer. Set aside for 20 minutes to allow the ginger to infuse. Return to the heat and bring back to a simmer. Remove from heat, strain out ginger and stir in the chocolate. Cool and store in the refrigerator.

Ginger Pastry Cream
Combine the vanilla bean, milk and ginger in a saucepan and bring to a simmer. Set aside for 20 minutes to allow the ginger to infuse. Return to the heat and bring to a simmer. Remove from heat and strain.
   Whisk the sugar and egg yolks together. Add the cornflour and flour and slowly whisk in the warm milk mixture. Pour the mixture back into the saucepan. Over a medium heat, bring to a simmer. Whisk constantly until the pastry cream is thick and shiny. Remove from heat, place pastry cream into an electric kitchen mixer and whisk on high until cooled. Store in the refrigerator in an airtight container.

GINGER SOUFFLÉ

15 g (½ oz) butter, softened

15 g (½ oz) caster (superfine) sugar

5 egg whites, at room temperature

30 g (1 oz) caster (superfine) sugar

1 squeeze lemon juice

30 g (1 oz) Ginger Pastry Cream, at room temperature

60 g (2 oz) Ginger Chocolate Ganache, cold

TO SERVE

15 g (½ oz) icing sugar

1 quantity Palm Sugar & Tamarind Ice Cream (see recipe)

Ginger Soufflé

Butter inside six 125 ml (4 fl oz) soufflé moulds. Dust over the buttered moulds with the 15 g (½ oz) of sugar. Preheat the oven to 170°C (335°F).

Whisk the egg whites on high until soft peaks form. Sprinkle in 30 g (1 oz) of sugar and the lemon juice and continue whisking until shiny, stiff meringue peaks just form.

Place the pastry cream into a large clean bowl and gently fold in the meringue.

Spoon one teaspoon of ginger chocolate ganache into the bottom centre of each mould. Spoon in the soufflé mixture, to above the tops of the moulds. With the back of a knife, level the mixture across the moulds. Run your thumb around the inside edge of each mould to clean the top rim.

Place in the oven and cook for 12–14 minutes or until soufflés have risen up at least 2 cm (¾ in) and have a lovely golden top. Opening the oven door to sneak a peak is fine—as long as you open and close the oven door quickly, the oven temperature will not drop dramatically enough to make the soufflés fall.

To Serve

Serve soufflés immediately from the oven, as they will begin to collapse as they cool. Lightly dust the soufflé tops with icing sugar and transfer to serving plates with the Palm Sugar and Tamarind Ice Cream.

YELLOW BEAN CINNAMON SPONGE, GINGER SPICED SYRUP

with coconut ginger sorbet

Makes 6 generous portions

YELLOW BEAN CINNAMON SPONGE

125 g (4 oz) mung beans (soaked overnight)
2 eggs, at room temperature
100 g (3½ oz) caster (superfine) sugar
170 ml (5½ fl oz) coconut cream
1 tablespoon (15 g) rice flour
½ teaspoon ground cinnamon

GINGER SPICED SYRUP

250 g (8½ oz) sugar
250 ml (8½ fl oz) water
2 cinnamon quills
1 vanilla bean, split lengthwise and scraped
10 pieces of fresh ginger, finely sliced

This gluten-free sponge is quite unusual, but is very light and tastes a little like banana. Delicious eaten on its own as a healthy afternoon treat. For entertaining, dress up the sponge with ginger spiced syrup, coconut cream and a scoop of Coconut Ginger Sorbet. ~ Nadine

Yellow Bean Cinnamon Sponge
Preheat oven to 180°C (350°F).

Drain beans and boil in salted water until very soft, strain well squeezing out all water then cool.

Beat eggs and sugar until triple in volume.

Add coconut cream to beans, place into blender and blend until smooth.

Fold sifted rice flour and cinnamon into egg mixture.

Fold in mung bean mix. Pour into a lined sponge tray approximately 50 cm (19½ in) x 20 cm (7¾ in).

Cook for 15–20 minutes until just lightly browned and knife comes out clean when tested. Let cool.

Ginger Spiced Syrup
Mix all the ingredients in a saucepan and bring to a boil.

Boil on high for about 5 minutes, until ginger is translucent.

When cool, remove cinnamon quills and vanilla bean.

COCONUT CREAM

250 ml (8½ fl oz) coconut
cream
30 g (1 oz) caster (superfine)
sugar
¼ teaspoon salt

TO SERVE

1 quantity Coconut Ginger
Sorbet (see recipe)
some Shaved Coconut (see
recipe)

Coconut Cream

Combine all ingredients in a saucepan and heat gently,
stirring until sugar and salt have dissolved.

To Serve

In a bowl or glass, pour in the coconut cream.
Place a slice of pudding on top of coconut cream.
Drizzle warm Ginger Spiced Syrup on top of the cake
and garnish with a scoop of Coconut Ginger Sorbet
and Shaved Coconut.

GINGER, NUT CARAMEL TART
with vanilla crème & chocolate shards

Makes 6 generous portions or 12 bite-sized nibbles

GINGER PASTRY

90 g (3 oz) pure icing (confectioners') sugar, sifted
80 g (2½ oz) almond meal
175 g (6 oz) unsalted butter, chopped and softened
2 egg yolks
125 g (4 oz) plain (all-purpose) flour, sifted
¼ teaspoon salt
25 g (¾ oz) ground ginger

NUT CARAMEL

220 g (7½ oz) butter
175 g (6 oz) dark palm sugar
250 ml (8½ fl oz) light corn syrup
1 x 395 g tin (13½ oz) sweetened condensed milk
15 g (½ oz) cocoa powder, sifted
80 ml (2½ fl oz) coffee liqueur
250 g (8½ oz) macadamia or Brazil nuts, roasted

This caramel treat is great for dessert, or just by itself as an afternoon tea nibble. This slice keeps well in the refrigerator for two to three days, so very handy when unexpected guests arrive. ~ Nadine

Ginger Pastry

Preheat oven to 170°C (325°F).

Put icing sugar, almond meal and butter into a mixing bowl with whisk attachment and beat on medium speed for 2–3 minutes or until mixture turns pale. Gradually add egg yolks, beating well between each addition. Fold in flour, salt and ground ginger until just combined.

Place dough on sheet of cling film, flatten dough to about 2 cm (¾ in) thick.

Place in refrigerator for two hours until dough has firmed.

Line a square 20–30 cm tin (8–12 in) with non-stick baking paper (lamington tin would be great).

Roll pastry out to about 6 mm (¼ in) thick and place onto the lined tray. Bake for 15–20 minutes or until pastry is golden. Remove from oven to cool.

Nut Caramel

Melt butter in saucepan over low heat. Add sugar and whisk until combined. Add corn syrup and condensed milk, increase heat to high and bring to the boil.

Whisking occasionally, cook for 10–12 minutes or until thick. (Make sure that the caramel is thick.)

VANILLA CRÈME
250 ml (8 fl oz) thickened
  cream
2 vanilla beans, halved and
  scraped (or 15 ml/ ½ fl oz
  vanilla extract)

TO SERVE
Chocolate Shards (see
  recipe)
icing (confectioners') sugar,
  for dusting

Remove from the heat and add cocoa powder, liqueur and nuts.

Pour caramel mix over pastry base. Refrigerate to set overnight. Cut into six rectangles (or smaller ones for nibbles).

Vanilla Crème
Place cream in a mixing bowl, add vanilla, beat until soft peaks form.

Place in refrigerator until needed.

To Serve
Cut caramel with a hot wet knife into desired size, place onto serving plate. Dollop with a spoon of Vanilla Crème and decorate with Chocolate Shards. If desired dust with pure icing sugar.

LEMONGRASS TART
with mango & kaffir lime meringue

Serves 6

PASTRY

125 g (4 oz) diced cold
    butter
75 g (2½ oz) icing
    (confectioners') sugar
2 egg yolks
250 g (9 oz) plain (all-
    purpose) flour (plus extra
    for kneading)
pinch salt
2 egg whites, to brush the
    cooked tart

Asian aromatics like lemongrass and kaffir lime really complement sweet dishes. With fresh eggs from my chickens mounting up, there is always an excuse to indulge in this dessert. ~ Renee

Pastry

In a food processor, combine butter and sugar, blending until creamy. Add egg yolks one at a time.

Add flour, pinch of salt and blend until pastry resembles breadcrumbs.

Flour surface of a clean bench, turn out pastry and knead until well combined.

Roll out between two pieces of greaseproof paper to 2–3 mm (1/8 in) thick. Rest dough in refrigerator for at least 30 minutes.

Grease six tart moulds about 9 cm (3½ in) diameter.

To cut six circles of pastry, find a cup or plate with a diameter of 13 cm (5 in) and trace around rim to get perfect circles.

Gently ease pastry into moulds. With a small knife, trim any overhanging pastry and with a fork, stab holes in the base.

Rest in refrigerator for 15 minutes.

Preheat oven to 180°C (350°F). Bake tart shells for 20 minutes or until pastry is cooked golden brown.

When tart shells come out and while still hot, brush the pastry with egg whites, which will seal all the holes.

Allow to cool then refrigerate until needed.

Lemongrass Filling

Place coconut cream, cream, split vanilla bean and bruised and chopped lemongrass (to bruise lemongrass, hit it hard with a meat mallet, pestle or the

LEMONGRASS FILLING

300 ml (10½ fl oz) coconut
    cream
200 ml (7 fl oz) thickened
    cream
1 vanilla bean, cut in
    half lengthwise and
    scraped
4 lemongrass stalks
2 egg yolks
100 g (3½ oz) caster
    (superfine) sugar
1 gelatine sheet

KAFFIR LIME MERINGUE

12 kaffir lime leaves
20 g (²/₃ oz) glucose syrup
80 g (2½ oz) caster
    (superfine) sugar
35 ml (1½ fl oz) water
2 egg whites

MANGO

1 large or 2 small mangos
    (tinned or frozen
    mango can be used,
    though fresh is best)

base of a heavy pot) into a saucepan and heat until just before it starts to simmer, then take off the heat and let it infuse for at least 30 minutes.

Whisk together egg yolks and sugar, then mix in infused cream. Soak gelatine in cold water.

Cook infused cream over double boiler (making sure water doesn't touch bowl) until it thickens to a spoon-coating consistency.

Drain water off gelatine and dissolve in heated cream. Strain mix through fine strainer, discard lemongrass and vanilla bean.

Pour mix into cooked tart shells and chill until set, about 3–4 hours.

Kaffir Lime Meringue

Remove stems from kaffir leaves then blend in a spice grinder until kaffir leaves are a fine powder and you have about a teaspoonful. Heat glucose syrup, sugar and water to 120°C (250°F) or until reaches hard ball stage (see Glossary).

In an electric mixer, beat egg whites to soft peaks, then with beaters on low, slowly pour in sugar syrup.

Turn beaters to high and continue beating until meringue has cooled. Meringue should be silky smooth and bright white.

Fold through powdered kaffir lime leaves.

Spoon into a piping bag and keep refrigerated until ready to use.

Mango

With a knife, peel mango, then slice on either side of seed to remove the cheeks. Finely slice mango cheeks until you have thin ribbons of mango. Store in refrigerator until needed.

To Serve

Place lemongrass tarts on six serving plates. Gently arrange the mango ribbons over top of tart. Pipe a small circle of meringue over the mango in centre of tart, leaving some mango visible on the edges.

With a brûlée torch, caramelise top of the meringue. Caramelising the meringue can be achieved under a hot grill, though you risk melting the tart filling.

PINEAPPLE TARTE TATIN
with vanilla & black pepper ice cream

Serves 6

70 g (2½ oz) caster
  (superfine) sugar
35 g (1¼ oz) butter
½ large pineapple, peeled
  and cut lengthways
1 sheet puff pastry

TO SERVE

1 quantity Vanilla & Black
  Pepper Ice Cream (see
  recipe)

This visually stunning, wonderfully sticky yet deliciously crisp tart, is unbelievably easy to make. Seriously! ~ Libby

Preheat oven to 190°C (375°F).

Place a straight-sided, ovenproof 24 cm (9½ in) frying pan over medium heat. Add 1 tablespoon of the sugar to the pan. Once the pan is warm enough to melt the sugar, sprinkle in the remaining sugar. Stir constantly with a wooden spoon until all the sugar has melted and is light brown in colour. As soon as the caramel begins to darken and slightly smoke, add the butter. Use a whisk to stir until well combined. Remove from heat and place aside for 5 minutes.

Lay the pineapple with its cut side on a chopping board. Slice across its length at 5 mm (¼ in) intervals. Lay the individual pineapple semi-circles flat on the board and cut out the core with a small pastry cutter.

Fan the pineapple slices over the caramel and around the frying pan, ensuring the pineapple is evenly arranged, with no gaps.

Using an upside-down, 25 cm (10 in) dinner plate as your guide, cut out a puff pastry disc. Lay the disc across the top of the pineapple, tucking the pastry edges down at the edges of the frying pan. Prick the pastry 4 times across its top.

Place the frying pan into the oven and cook for 20 minutes, or until the puff pastry has browned. Remove the tarte tatin from the oven and allow to sit for 5 minutes.

Place a plate that is larger than the frying pan's diameter on top and quickly flip over the frying pan. This needs to be done really quickly to stop the hot caramel from spilling out the sides.

To Serve
Transfer your warm pineapple tarte tatin to a serving board. Portion at the dining table and serve each slice with a scoop of Vanilla and Black Pepper Ice Cream.

DECONSTRUCTED CITRUS PISTACHIO TART
with lemongrass granita

Serves 6

CITRUS CURD
5 egg yolks
100 g (3½ oz) caster
    (superfine) sugar
125 ml (4 fl oz) lime juice
150 ml (5 fl oz) cream
25 g (¾ oz) butter, cubed

PISTACHIO SHORTBREAD
200 g (7 oz) plain (all-
    purpose) flour
¼ teaspoon salt
125 g (4 oz) unsalted butter,
    softened
90 g (3 oz) caster (superfine)
    sugar
1 egg, beaten
50 g (1¾ oz) pistachio nuts,
    roasted and chopped

TO SERVE
1 quantity Lemongrass
    Granita (see recipe)
1 quantity Lemon Candy
    (see recipe)

This delicious summer dessert is stunning to the eye if served in a martini glass or brandy balloon. ~ Nadine.

Citrus Curd
Whisk egg yolks and sugar in a heatproof bowl until sugar has dissolved. Add lime juice and cream.

Place bowl over a saucepan of boiling water and whisk until thick, about 8–10 minutes. Then whisk in butter.

Cool at room temperature.

Pistachio Shortbread
Preheat the oven to 160°C (320°F).
Sift the flour and salt into a medium-sized bowl.

In a large bowl, cream the butter and sugar until smooth and creamy. Gradually work in the egg. Fold in the flour and the cooled nuts.

Roll into a ball, wrap in cling film and refrigerate for 20 minutes.

Line a baking tray with baking sheet and roll out dough onto it, about 1 cm (¼ in) thickness.

Bake for 10–15 minutes or until golden brown. Let cool, then gently blitz in a kitchen blender until roughly chopped.

To Serve
Place a generous tablespoon of Citrus Curd in the base of a glass. Sprinkle with crushed shortbread, then a layer of Lemongrass Granita and garnish with Lemon Candy.

POACHED PEACHES
with spiced butter biscuits & chilled ginger custard

Serves 6

SPICED BUTTER BISCUITS
100 g (3½ oz) butter, softened
90 g (3 oz) icing (confectioners') sugar, sifted
1 egg yolk
170 g (6 oz) plain (all-purpose) flour
1 teaspoon ground cinnamon
1 teaspoon ground ginger
pinch salt

CHILLED GINGER CUSTARD
75 g (2½ oz) caster (superfine) sugar
40 ml (1½ fl oz) water
6 egg yolks
½ titanium gelatine sheet (see Glossary)
70 ml (2⅓ fl oz) ginger wine
150 ml (5 fl oz) cream

Deliciously light and perfumed, these poached peaches will sweeten up any dessert. Here I've matched the fruit with buttery fragrant spices and creamy ginger custard. Enjoy seasonal peaches while that warm summer feeling is in the air. ~ Libby

Spiced Butter Biscuits
Blitz butter and sugar in a food processor until combined. Add egg yolk and continue processing.

Sift together flour, spices and salt and add to the food processor. When dough starts to come together, turn it out onto a kitchen bench and knead into a ball. Flatten ball, wrap with cling film and rest in the refrigerator for 30 minutes.

Preheat oven to 190°C (375°F) and line an oven tray with baking paper.

Remove pastry and place between two sheets of baking paper. Roll it out to 3 mm (⅛ in) thickness. Rest in the refrigerator for another 20 minutes.

Using a 7½ cm (3 in) round cookie cutter, cut out 12 circles from the flattened pastry.

Place circles on a lined baking tray and bake for 10–15 minutes or until golden brown. Cool on tray.

Store in an airtight container, away from any moisture for 2 days. Unused biscuit dough can be kept wrapped in the freezer for 1 month.

Chilled Ginger Custard
Place sugar and water into a small saucepan and bring to a boil over medium heat.

Place yolks in bowl with an electric whisk attached.

When the sugar syrup reaches 118°C (245°F) on a sugar

POACHED PEACHES

250 ml (8½ fl oz) orange juice
250 ml (8½ fl oz) water
250 g (9 oz) light palm sugar, grated
2 cinnamon quills
15 g (½ oz) ginger, thinly sliced
½ vanilla bean, split lengthwise
8 peaches, halved and stone removed

TO SERVE

15 g (½ oz) icing (confectioners') sugar
12 mint leaves, baby tips

thermometer, remove from heat and pour over the whisking yolks in a thin continuous stream. Whisk on high until mixture is cold.

Soften the gelatine sheet in cold water.

Heat ginger wine in a small saucepan to a simmer, remove from heat. Squeeze excess water from gelatine and add to the saucepan, stirring to dissolve. Strain liquid into a bowl and cool.

Whisk the ginger wine mixture into the cold egg mixture.

Whisk the cream to soft peaks. Lightly fold through the ginger egg mix. Place in refrigerator to set.

Poached Peaches

Combine the juice, water, sugar, cinnamon, ginger and vanilla bean in a large frying pan and bring to a simmer over a low heat, stirring to dissolve the sugar.

Place peaches into the poaching liquid, cut side up. Allow liquid to return to a simmer. Test peaches for doneness by piercing a small knife through the centre. Remove with a slotted spoon when the peaches are just cooked.

Once the peaches have cooled, peel away their skins and store covered with the cool poaching liquid in an airtight container in the refrigerator for up to 3 days.

To Serve

Dust a Spiced Butter Biscuit with icing sugar, place into the centre of each serving plate. Slice the peaches into thick wedges and arrange a few on top of each biscuit. Spoon chilled ginger custard over the peaches. Repeat with another layer of biscuits, peaches and custard on top. Scatter a few mint tips over each dessert.

LYCHEE BRÛLÉE
with raspberry swirl

Serves 6–8 in small glasses

200 g (7 oz) frozen
    raspberries
1 can lychees in syrup,
    reserving 100 ml
    (3½ fl oz) of the lychee
    syrup
100 g (3½ oz) palm sugar
1 vanilla bean
500 ml (16 fl oz) pure cream
6 egg yolks
60 g (2 oz) caster (superfine)
    sugar
30 ml (1 fl oz) lychee liqueur
2 gelatine sheets
2–3 tablespoons raspberry
    jam (reserved from frozen
    raspberries)

This brûlée is not only sweet and fruity but is visually colourful, making it the perfect finish to a dinner party. You can make it the day before, store it in the refrigerator, and finish with the toffee topping just before serving. Too easy! ~ Renee

Pick through raspberries and remove 50 g (1¾ oz) of large whole raspberries to use as garnish. Place berries on paper towel in a container to defrost in refrigerator. Save the other 150 g (5 oz) raspberries to make the raspberry jam for the swirl.

Slice 50 g (1¾ oz) of the tinned lychees and keep them for garnish. Make sure you don't discard the syrup as it is needed in the brûlée mix.

Break up palm sugar and place in a small saucepan with 150 g (5 oz) of frozen raspberries and cook on a medium heat until sugar dissolves and raspberries break down. Remove from heat and pass through a fine strainer. Set aside to cool.

Split vanilla bean and add to the cream in a saucepan and heat to just before boiling point. Remove from heat and allow to infuse for 10–15 minutes.

Whisk together egg yolks and sugar, pour in cooled cream, lychee liqueur and the lychee syrup from the tinned lychees. Whisk until combined.

Soak gelatine in cold water. Over a double boiler, stir brûlée mix until it coats the back of a spoon. This should be quite thick. Remove from heat. Strain water off the gelatine and add gelatine to brûlée mix, stirring until dissolved. Strain brûlée mix and discard vanilla bean.

Pour brûlée into 6–8 small glasses about 120 ml (4 fl

TO SERVE

caster (superfine) sugar, for caramelising the brûlée
mint leaves for garnish

oz) and place in refrigerator for 5–10 minutes until just starting to set.

Pour about 1–2 teaspoons of raspberry jam onto each brûlée and, using a skewer, gently stir, being careful not to mix too much because you want a raspberry swirl effect. Refrigerate to set completely—at least 3–4 hours, but preferably overnight.

To Serve

Sprinkle top of each brûlée with caster sugar and with a brûlée torch, melt sugar to toffee. It is not recommended to use a grill for this brûlée as it will melt the gelatine. If slight melting does occur, place brûlée back in refrigerator for 10 minutes to re-set.

Place brûlée glass on serving plate with a side salad using the reserved lychees, raspberries and garnish with tiny mint leaves or finely sliced mint.

This brûlée could also be garnished with Honey Wafers (see recipe).

PASSIONFRUIT COCONUT BRÛLÉE
with sesame tuile

Serves 6

115 g (3¾ oz) caster
    (superfine) sugar
4 eggs
1 vanilla bean
340 ml (11½ fl oz) coconut
    cream
40 ml (1½ fl oz) milk
125 ml (4 fl oz) passionfruit
    pulp

TO SERVE

caster (superfine) sugar, to
    caramelise the brûlée
1 quantity Sesame Tuile (see
    recipe)
icing (confectioners') sugar,
    to dust

Brûlées are one of my favourite desserts. The combination of sweet creamy coconut and the refreshing zing of passionfruit makes this one a winner. ~ Renee

Whisk together sugar and eggs.

Split vanilla bean down the centre and scrape out seeds. Add seeds to sugar and eggs. Whisk in coconut cream and milk.

Strain excess liquid off passionfruit pulp, then add the liquid to mix.

Pour mix into six small ramekins, 6 cm (2½ in) diameter, or into Chinese tea cups.

In a baking tray with large sides, lay a mesh cleaning cloth on the bottom. Place the ramekins on the cloth and fill the baking tray with hot tap water three-quarters of the way up the sides of the ramekin. Cover tray with foil and cook in a 150°C (300°F) oven for 30 minutes or until brûlée is cooked. It will still have a slight wobble to it. Remove from tray and cool completely in refrigerator. Best if refrigerated overnight.

To Serve

Sprinkle a thin layer of caster sugar on top of brûlée. Using a brûlée torch, melt sugar until caramelised.

If you don't have a torch, place brûlée under a hot grill until sugar has melted. This method does tend to soften the brûlée though and will change the consistency.

Place brûlée on desired serving plate. Dust Sesame Tuile with icing sugar and place on the side to add a lovely texture contrast.

BANANA CRÈME BRÛLÉE
with vanilla bean syrup
& raspberry, papaya, coconut salad

Serves 6

VANILLA BEAN SYRUP

125 g (¼ lb) caster
(superfine) sugar
5 g (¼ oz) glucose syrup
125 ml (4 fl oz) water
½ vanilla bean, split
lengthways

RASPBERRY, PAPAYA, COCONUT SALAD

5 g (¼ oz) Asian basil seeds
(available at Asian
supermarkets)
25 ml (¾ fl oz) cold water
100 g (3½ oz) coconut zest
(see recipe)
¼ papaya
200 g (7 oz) raspberries

BANANA CRÈME BRÛLÉE

500 ml (16 fl oz) cream
½ vanilla bean
2 bananas, mashed
90 g (3 oz) caster (superfine)
sugar
5 egg yolks

Tap, tap, tap, then crack—and you're through that beautiful golden glaze into the creamy banana below. May you enjoy this delicious brûlée moment, many times over. ~ Libby

Vanilla Bean Syrup

Place sugar, glucose syrup and water into a heavy-based saucepan. Place over a medium heat and bring to a simmer. Once the sugar has dissolved, add the vanilla bean. Remove from the heat and allow to cool down. Keep stored in your refrigerator.

Raspberry, Papaya, Coconut Salad

Soak the basil seeds in the cold water. Within a couple of minutes they will have a translucent coating surrounding them. This is what you want.

Zest some fresh coconut. See the recipe in the Bling section on how to zest a coconut.

Peel the quarter of papaya, cut it in half lengthways and scoop out the seeds. Lay cut side down, and thinly slice.

Keep the fruit salad ingredients covered in the refrigerator until you are ready to serve.

Banana Crème Brûlée

Preheat the oven to 120°C (250°F).

Combine cream, vanilla bean, banana and 45 g (1½ oz) of the sugar into a saucepan. Place over a medium heat and bring to a simmer. Remove from heat and allow to sit for 20 minutes for the flavours to infuse. Return saucepan

154

TO SERVE

45 g (1½ oz) caster (superfine) sugar, extra for brûlée top

to the heat and return to a simmer. Take off the heat, strain and discard the solids.

Whisk together the egg yolks and remaining 45 g (1½ oz) of sugar until pale and slightly thickened. Slowly whisk in the warm banana cream mix. Strain the mixture into a pouring jug.

Flatten a damp tea towel into the base of a deep-sided baking tray. On top, place six 100 ml (2¾ oz) soufflé moulds and fill with the warm banana custard mixture. Pour hot water into the tray so that the water comes three-quarters of the way up the sides of the moulds.

Transfer the tray to the middle shelf in your oven. Cook for 45 minutes, or until the crèmes are just set around the edges and wobble in the centre when you gently tap them. Remove from oven, remove from water bath and refrigerate until they are chilled.

To Serve

Place the sliced papaya, coconut zest and 2 teaspoons of soaked basil seeds into a bowl and spoon over enough Vanilla Bean Syrup to coat the fruit when gently tossed.

Take the brûlées out of the refrigerator, sprinkle each with the remaining 45 g (1½ oz) sugar. Using a small kitchen blowtorch, caramelise the sugar tops. Place each brûlée into the centre of your six serving plates. Stack a small amount of the fruit salad mix on top of each brûlée and garnish with the raspberries.

CINNAMON & COFFEE BRÛLÉE

Serves 6

300 ml (10½ fl oz) whipping
    cream
150 ml (5 fl oz) milk
75 g (2½ oz) caster
    (superfine) sugar
3 cinnamon quills
40 ml (1½ fl oz) espresso
    coffee
9 medium egg yolks

I really love crème brûlée and this is one that I often make. It brings back fond memories of hanging out in cafés, lapping up the coffee culture. ~ Nathan

Preheat oven to 110°C (230°F).

Place the cream, milk, sugar, cinnamon and espresso into a medium-sized pan. On a low heat slowly bring the mixture to a boil, stirring frequently until the sugar is dissolved. Set aside for 20 minutes to let the cinnamon infuse. Bring the mixture back to the boil. Strain the mixture through a fine sieve and, a little at a time, whisk the mixture into the eggs. Strain through a fine strainer to remove any remaining egg particles that may have scrambled. Pour into desired serving dishes such as coffee cups or soufflé moulds.

Place the moulds into a deep baking tray and pour hot water into the baking tray until it reaches about halfway up the moulds. Bake for 30 minutes and then check them and turn the tray around. Bake for a further 10 minutes; when ready the crèmes should still be slightly wobbly. Remove from the oven and allow to cool in the water-filled tray. Refrigerate for at least a couple of hours or until required to serve.

To Serve
Sprinkle a generous amount of caster (superfine) sugar evenly onto each crème brûlée and, with a blowtorch or under a really hot grill, caramelise the sugar. If you choose, serve with some honey wafers or tuiles or maybe even some chocolate truffles.

CHOCOLATE BRÛLÉE with CHILLI RASPBERRY JAM, CHILLI CANDY
& chocolate brandy snap

Serves 6

CHOCOLATE BRÛLÉE
8 egg yolks
75 g (2½ oz) caster (superfine)
    sugar
500 ml (16 fl oz) cream
1 vanilla bean, cut in half
    lengthways and scraped
150 g (5oz) dark chocolate,
    chopped
extra sugar for caramelising

CHILLI RASPBERRY JAM
5 long red chillies (deseeded)
250 g (8½ oz) frozen
    raspberries
250 g (8½ oz) palm sugar

TO SERVE
some strips of Chilli Candy
    (see recipe)
6 Chocolate Brandy Snaps
    (see recipe)

A dessert menu favourite—lush silken chocolate, burnt sugar, splash of raspberry and chilli. What more could you desire? ~ Nadine

Chocolate Brûlée
Whisk eggs and sugar in a heatproof bowl until thick and creamy.

Pour cream into a saucepan, add vanilla bean and bring to just on boiling point.

Pour onto egg mix and whisk well, pour back into saucepan and stir over low heat until the mix looks very thick and a bit like scrambled eggs.

Take off the heat and whisk in chocolate. Remove vanilla bean.

Blend mix with a stick blender until smooth and glossy, then pass through a fine strainer.

Chilli Raspberry Jam
Blend chillies in a food processor, then add to raspberries and palm sugar in a saucepan. Bring to a simmer and cook on low heat for half an hour or until a thick jam. Cool.

To Serve
Place 1 teaspoon of raspberry chilli jam on the bottom of each ramekin. Fill with the chocolate mix.

Sprinkle 1 tablespoon of sugar on top of each brûlée. Fire up a blowtorch and caramelise the sugar.

Garnish with some strips of Chilli Candy on top of the cooled sugar. Serve with a Chocolate Brandy Snap on side of the plate.

MANGO MERINGUE
with raspberry champagne jellies

Makes 5–6 small meringues

MERINGUE
3 large egg whites
115 g (3¾ oz) caster
    (superfine) sugar
5-6 120 ml (4 fl oz) Chinese
    tea cups for moulds

MANGO PUREE
100 g (3½ oz) fresh mango
1 teaspoon (5 g) citric acid
1 pinch salt
½ lime, juiced
110 g (3½ oz) sugar
NB: The lime and salt
    amounts are only a guide
    as mangoes vary in
    sweetness.

TO SERVE
tropical fruits, such as
    mango, passionfruit,
    banana, etc for garnish
1 quantity Raspberry
    Champagne Jelly, sliced
    (see recipe)
mint sprigs, for garnish

I created this summer dessert for a New Year's Eve menu—a sublime way to finish another busy year at Spirit House. ~ Nathan

Meringue
Preheat the oven to 130°C (275°F). Over a double boiler, whisk the egg whites and caster sugar until the sugar is completely dissolved and the egg whites slightly warm.

Transfer to electric mixer and whisk to soft peaks.

Place the greased tea cups filled with the meringue mixture in a water bath and cover with foil. Cook in the oven for 20 minutes, remove from water bath and refrigerate in their moulds for at least an hour.

Mango Puree
Place all ingredients in a blender and blitz until it resembles a fine puree. Pass through a fine sieve. Keep in mind that the meringue is quite sweet, so the mango mixture needs to be a little sour.

To Serve
With a melon baller, scoop out the bottom and middle of the meringue. Reserve the scooped out meringue.

Fill hole with mango puree, leaving a little room to patch up the hole with reserved meringue so that the puree won't come out. Turn out onto a serving plate. Arrange diced tropical fruits and slices of Raspberry Champagne Jelly around the meringue. Garnish with mint sprigs and a drizzle of mango puree.

WHITE CHOCOLATE, GINGER PISTACHIO

meringues, whipped cream, dark palm caramel & pistachio praline

Serves 6

DARK PALM CARAMEL
20 g (²/₃ oz) butter
150 g (5 oz) dark palm sugar, grated
180 ml (6 fl oz) cream

WHIPPED CREAM
15 g (½ oz) icing (confectioners') sugar, sifted
250 ml (8½ fl oz) cream

WHITE CHOCOLATE, GINGER & PISTACHIO MERINGUES
55 g (2 oz) white chocolate, chopped
35 g (1¼ oz) pistachio nuts, shelled and chopped
15 g (½ oz) stem ginger, finely chopped
15 g (½ oz) caster (superfine) sugar
1 egg white, at room temperature
50 g (1¾ oz) caster (superfine) sugar

These individual meringues can be eaten at room temperature when they're lovely, light and crisp— or straight from the oven when the chocolate is all gooey. This recipe yields nine meringues, so should any happen to go 'missing' after baking, no one will notice. ~ Libby

Dark Palm Caramel
Place all ingredients into a saucepan and bring to a simmer over medium heat. Stir constantly, to combine well.

Remove from heat, strain and cool to room temperature. Keep stored in an airtight container in your refrigerator for up to 2 weeks.

Whipped Cream
In a cold bowl, whisk the sugar and the cream together until soft peaks form. Keep covered in refrigerator until it is ready to serve.

White Chocolate, Ginger & Pistachio Meringue
Combine chocolate, pistachio nuts and ginger in a bowl and toss thoroughly with the 15 g (½ oz) of sugar.

Preheat oven to 120°C (250°F). Line an oven tray with baking paper.

Place the egg white into the bowl of an electric mixer. Whisk on high speed until the egg white holds soft peaks. Sprinkle in the remaining 50 g (1¾ oz) sugar. Continue whisking on high speed until the mix becomes shiny and just holds firm peaks.

Carefully fold one-third of the chocolate, ginger and

TO SERVE

1 quantity Pistachio Praline
(see recipe)

nut mix into the meringue. Once it is fully incorporated, follow with the next one-third, then the last one-third, folding slowly and thoroughly.

Using a 5 cm (2 in) round cutter dipped in warm water, spoon your meringue mix out onto the oven tray. Remember to leave enough space between each meringue for expansion during cooking.

Bake meringues for 20 minutes, then reduce the oven temperature to 70°C (160°F) and bake for a further 40 minutes, or until crisp and dry. Remove from oven and allow to cool on the tray. Keep stored in an airtight container, away from any moisture for 3 days.

To Serve

Place each meringue into the centre of the six serving plates. Spoon a large dollop of Whipped Cream on top of each meringue. Drizzle a little Dark Palm Caramel across the cream. With a sharp knife, roughly chop some Pistachio Praline and scatter across the top and around the sides of the meringues.

Fresh cherries, bananas, passionfruit, peaches, plums, tropical fruits and chocolate would all be wonderful accompaniments.

PASSIONFRUIT MARSHMALLOW,
raspberry, peanut praline, rocky road smear

Serves 6

PASSIONFRUIT MARSHMALLOW

500 g (17½ oz) white sugar
15 g (½ oz) glucose syrup
150 ml (5½ fl oz) water
4 gelatine sheets
150 ml (5½ fl oz) strained
    passionfruit juice
3 egg whites
100 g (3½ oz) icing
    (confectioners') sugar
100 g (3½ oz) cornflour
    (cornstarch)
3 drops yellow food colour

CHOCOLATE GANACHE

100 ml (2¼ fl oz) thickened
    cream
225 g (8 oz) dark chocolate

This delicious rendition of 'rocky road' can be served on individual plates or set into a slab. Keep in a secret hiding place—otherwise it will quickly disappear. Read the whole recipe before you start, as there are a few more garnish ingredients in the 'To Serve' section. ~ Nadine

Passionfruit Marshmallow

Stir 400 g (14 oz) sugar, glucose syrup, 150 ml (5 fl oz) water in a small pan over low heat, until sugar dissolves.

Bring to boil until the mixture reaches 121°C (250°F) on a sugar thermometer.

Soften gelatine in cold water for 2–3 minutes, squeeze out excess water.

Bring passionfruit juice to the boil in a small pan, remove from the heat and stir in gelatine until dissolved.

Using an electric mixer, whisk egg whites to soft peaks, then gradually add remaining 100 g (3½ oz) white sugar and whisk to firm peaks. Still whisking gently, pour in hot sugar syrup down the side of the bowl in a thin stream. Continue whisking until mixture thickens. Then, on lowest mixer setting, pour in passionfruit and gelatine mix and the drops of yellow food colour.

Line a 20 cm x 30 cm (7¾ x 11¾ in) slice tin with baking paper. Sift together the icing sugar and cornflour and dust the lined tray with 2 tablespoons of the mixture.

Spoon in marshmallow mixture, and dust the top with 2 tablespoons of the cornflour/icing sugar mixture.

TO SERVE

250 g (9 oz) punnet of
    raspberries
100 g (3½ oz) candied
    ginger, cut into small
    cubes
½ quantity Peanut Praline
    (see recipe)
45 g (1½ oz) shredded
    coconut, toasted
4 kaffir lime leaves, very
    finely chopped

Allow to cool in a cool dry place for 2 hours until set. Cover with cling film. When ready to serve, remove cling film and cut with a hot dry knife. Sprinkle more of the cornflour/sugar mix on top.

Chocolate Ganache

Bring cream to the boil. Pour over broken up chocolate, stir until combined and smooth. Leave to cool, but not set.

To Serve

Place a smear of the Chocolate Ganache on each plate. Place small cubes of marshmallow randomly on top of the ganache. Scatter raspberries, ginger and sprinkle with crumbled Peanut Praline. Top with toasted coconut and kaffir lime leaf.

For the slab

You will need a double batch of the ganache for this slab. Line a lamington tray or a tray 33 cm (13 in) x 23 cm (9 in) x 5 cm (2 in) with baking paper.

Pour half the ganache into tray, place all other ingredients as above. Then pour more of the ganache on top.

COCONUT MERINGUE
with passionfruit cream & seasonal fruits

Serves 6

COCONUT MERINGUE
4 egg whites, at room
    temperature
270 g (9½ oz) caster
    (superfine) sugar
½ teaspoon (2.5 ml) white
    vinegar
15 g (½ oz) cornflour
    (cornstarch)
½ teaspoon (2.5 ml) vanilla
    extract
50 g (1¾ oz) desiccated
    coconut

PASSIONFRUIT CREAM
8 ripe passionfruit
150 g (5oz) mascarpone
150 ml (5 fl oz) whipping
    cream
30 g (1 oz) icing
    (confectioners') sugar

TO SERVE
½ quantity of Pistachio
    Praline (see recipe)
6 Chocolate Shards (see
    recipe)

*Tiny, one-bite pillows with tangy passionfruit
and your choice of seasonal fruit. And, perhaps,
a naughty addition of Chocolate Shards or
Pistachio Praline … delicious. ~ Nadine*

Coconut Meringue
Preheat oven to 110°C (230°F).
    Whisk egg whites to soft peaks, then gradually add sugar.
Keep whisking on high until mix is very thick and glossy, and
sugar has dissolved. Fold in vinegar, cornflour, vanilla and
coconut.
    Line a sponge tray about 50 cm (19½ in) x 20 cm (7¾ in)
with baking paper. Place a greased cookie cutter on the
tray. Place mix into a piping bag and pipe the mix into the
cookie cutter. Lift up the cutter releasing the meringue. Re-
grease the cutter and repeat process until all mix is used.
    Bake for 20 minutes. Lower temperature to 70°C (160°F)
and cook for a further 15 minutes.

Passionfruit Cream
Puree passionfruit pulp in a blender. Boil puree in a small
pan until mixture is reduced by half, should take about 5
minutes. Pass through a sieve, cool, cover and chill.
    Mix the passionfruit puree into the mascarpone.
    Whip the cream and icing sugar to soft peaks, then fold
into passionfruit mixture. Chill.

To Serve
Place meringue on serving plate with a dollop of
passionfruit cream, some slices of fresh seasonal fruit
and, if desired, a garnish of Pistachio Praline or Chocolate
Shards.

POACHED MERINGUE
with basil ice cream & watermelon granita

Serves 8

POACHED MERINGUE
300 g (11 oz) egg white
300 g (11 oz) caster
(superfine) sugar

MALTOSE TUILES
100 g (3 ½ oz) caster
(superfine) sugar
200 g (7 oz) liquid maltose
(see Glossary. Glucose
syrup or honey can be
used in place of the
maltose if you can't find
it)
20 g (½ oz) flaked almonds

TO SERVE
Cheat's Basil Ice Cream (see
recipe)
Watermelon Granita (see
recipe)

This is a dessert that I was keen to make after being inspired by the great chef, Peter Gilmore. It's a play on Peter's well-known 'Snow Egg', although I have simplified it quite a bit so that it is achievable without hours of preparation.
~ Nathan

Poached Meringue
For this recipe, you will need a 6 cm (2¼ in) diameter, half hemisphere, silicon mould sheet. Whisk the egg whites until they form soft peaks and slowly add the sugar. Once the meringue forms firm peaks and the sugar has dissolved, place the meringue into 16 half-hemisphere moulds.

Cook the meringue in a baking tray large enough to hold the silicon mat and enough water to fill the bottom of the tray, in a preheated 120°C (250°F) oven for approximately 15 minutes. Allow to cool then un-mould the half hemispheres and store in the refrigerator on a baking paper lined tray until needed.

Maltose Tuiles
Heat the sugar and maltose together until it reaches a golden toffee colour (hard crack stage). Add the flaked almonds and immediately pour the mixture onto a tray lined with baking paper. Allow to cool completely. Process the hard caramel in a food processor to form a fine powder.

In a coarse sieve, add the praline mixture and sieve onto a tray lined with baking paper in a generous layer. Melt this mixture in a moderate oven until it forms a clear liquid paste. Remove from the oven and before the praline becomes too hard, cut into a 15 cm (6 in) diameter circle using a metal circle cutter. When each circle is hard, store between baking paper in an airtight container.

To Serve

Use a teaspoon to scoop out the centre of the half-hemisphere meringues, being careful not to break through the sides. Scoop some Basil Ice Cream small enough to fit into the meringues and top with another half-hemisphere meringue. Place the maltose tuile over the top of the meringues and using a blowtorch, melt the tuile so it is neatly moulded around the meringue.

Serve in a glass or on a plate, dust the meringue with icing sugar and serve with the Watermelon Granita. In the photo, I have also used some tropical fruits dressed with lime juice, icing sugar and finely sliced basil.

LEMON & COCONUT COOKIES

Serves 6

200 g (7 oz) butter, soft
220 g (7½ oz) caster
    (superfine) sugar
1 egg
175 g (6 oz) self-raising (self-
    rising) flour, sieved
110 g (3¾ oz) desiccated
    coconut
½ lemon, zest
½ lemon, juice

Add a platter of these lovely fresh baked cookies to bring a zing to your next tea party. ~ Libby

Cream the butter and sugar in an electric beater and until pale and creamy. Add the egg and mix until well combined.

Turn the mixer speed down to low and add the flour and coconut, alternating each a tablespoon at a time, and finishing with the flour. Now add the lemon zest and juice and beat until well incorporated.

Once the mix is starting to come away from the sides of the bowl, stop the mixer and turn the cookie dough out onto your bench top. If the dough seems too sticky to turn out, simply add an extra couple of tablespoons of self-raising flour into the mixer until the dough is firmer. Roll the dough into 2 × 4 cm (¾ x 1½ in) diameter cylinder, cover in cling film and place in the refrigerator to rest for 1 hour.

Preheat your oven to 160°C (325°F).

Remove one cookie dough cylinder from refrigerator and slice it across ways at 1 cm (½ in) intervals. This will yield 18 cookies. Lay the cookies flat on a tray lined with baking paper and bake in the oven for 20 minutes, or until cooked and golden. Remove from oven and transfer the cookies to a cake rack to cool.

Once the cookies have cooled, store them in an airtight container, away from any moisture for up to 4 days. The remaining cookie dough cylinder will keep for 5 days in the refrigerator or up to 2 weeks in the freezer.

LEMONGRASS GINGER BISCUITS

Makes 20

35 g (1¼ oz) butter
35 g (1¼ oz) grated palm
    sugar
¼ teaspoon cardamom
¼ teaspoon cinnamon
1 egg yolk
15 g (½ oz) lemongrass, finely
    sliced
15 g (½ oz) candied ginger
    finely chopped
60 g (2 oz) plain (all-purpose)
    flour

*Lovely to nibble with tea or coffee, or dust
with icing sugar and use as a garnish for my
White Chocolate Chai Mousse—creates such an
interesting texture and taste contrast. ~ Renee*

Beat butter, sugar and spices until creamy, then add
egg yolk and mix through.

Stir in lemongrass and ginger, and then fold in
sifted flour.

Turn mix out onto a floured surface, knead until well
combined and smooth.

Roll out between greaseproof papers to 5 mm (¹/8
in) thick, allow to rest in refrigerator for at least 30
minutes.

Preheat oven to 160°C (325°F).

Line a tray with greaseproof paper, cut biscuit mix
into 7½ x 3 cm (3 x 1½ in) rectangles, then diagonally
to create triangles. Place on tray and bake for 10–15
minutes or until just starting to colour.

CARDAMOM SPICED SHORTBREAD
with cashews & chocolate orange blossom filling

Makes about 25

BISCUIT DOUGH

125 g (4 oz) unsalted butter

500 g (17½ oz) self-raising (self-rising) flour

165 g (5½ oz) caster (superfine) sugar

1 whole egg

150 g (5 oz) sour cream

pinch salt

¼ teaspoon baking powder

¼ teaspoon ground cardamom

CASHEWS & CHOCOLATE ORANGE BLOSSOM FILLING

250 g (9 oz) toasted unsalted cashews

2 oranges, zested

150 g (5 oz) dark chocolate pieces

½ teaspoon orange blossom water

2 egg yolks to bind

1 extra egg for brushing

dust of icing (confectioners') sugar

An old Italian recipe tweaked to offer a taste of Asia. These will keep for a week in an airtight container. Share them with a friend over a strong coffee. ~ Nadine

Biscuit Dough

Preheat oven to 150°C (300°F).

Rub butter into flour until it resembles breadcrumbs. Then add sugar, egg, sour cream, salt, baking powder and cardamom. Mix well to form a dough. Place in refrigerator for 20 minutes. Roll out dough into a circle and cut into eighths, just like a pizza.

Cashews & Chocolate Orange Blossom Filling

Blend cashews until they form a thick paste, add orange zest, chocolate pieces, orange blossom water and egg yolks.

Place a teaspoon of mixture on the wide edge of each shortbread section and roll up so that they look like mini croissants.

Brush with extra beaten egg and bake for 15 minutes or until just starting to brown. Dust with icing sugar.

TRIO OF MACARONS

Makes about 40

MACARON CASES

125 g (4½ oz) ground
    almonds
225 g (8 oz) icing sugar
4 medium egg whites
1 pinch cream of tartar
25 g (1 oz) caster (superfine)
    sugar
food colourings of your
    choice

DARK CHOCOLATE CHILLI FILLING

150 g (5½ oz) pouring
    (whipping) cream
3 birds eye chillies (halved)
200 g (7 oz) dark chocolate,
    chopped or buttons
60 g (2¼ oz) unsalted butter,
    softened

MILK CHOCOLATE AND MINT FILLING

150 g (5½ oz) pouring
    (whipping) cream
½ bunch mint (leaves only)
200 g (7 oz) milk chocolate,
    chopped or buttons
60 g (2¼ oz) unsalted butter,
    softened

Macarons are so versatile and the list of colours and flavours is endless. To get the desired shade, use colouring gels rather than liquid, which alters the macaron texture. Colouring gels can be bought on the internet or from cake decorating shops. ~ Nathan

Macaron Cases

Preheat the oven to 180°C (350°F). Sift the almond meal and icing sugar together into bowl, then divide into three even amounts (preferably weighed). Using a freestanding electric mixer, whisk the eggs until they are just foamy and add the cream of tartar, then whisk to soft peaks. Reduce the speed and add the caster sugar, then return to a high speed and whisk until meringue is firm.

Remove the bowl from the machine and divide your meringue into separate amounts (preferably weighed). Colour the meringues into your desired colours, then fold each of the three almond meal and icing sugar mixtures into each of the coloured meringue mixes. The mix should be shiny and smooth.

Using a piping bag with a 1 cm (½ in) plain piping nozzle, pipe the mixture onto a baking tray lined with baking paper. The macarons should be about 2 cm (¾ in) in diameter, with 2.5 cm (1 in) between each one. Tap the tray from the bottom a few times to flatten the mixture slightly. Leave the macarons for 15–20 minutes to form a skin (this is how you will get the macarons to rise away from the base and give them that textured appearance on the bottom) then bake them in the centre of the oven with the door slightly ajar to let the

20 ml (¾ fl oz) peppermint
    essence

GINGER AND WHITE CHOCOLATE FILLING

150 g (5½ oz) pouring
    (whipping) cream
30 g (1 oz) freshly grated
    ginger
200 g (7 oz) white chocolate,
    chopped or buttons
60 g (2¼ oz) unsalted butter,
    softened

steam escape. Remove from the oven and leave to cool for 5 minutes before removing them from baking paper. Allow to cool completely before filling them.

Once the macaron cases are baked, they keep well for up to 3 months in the freezer provided they are in an airtight container and stored carefully.

Filling Method

Put the cream and the flavour (chilli, mint or ginger) into a saucepan over a low heat and let it come to a simmer slowly. Once it is simmering, remove from the heat and allow the flavouring ingredient to infuse for ten minutes. Return to the heat to warm the cream up again. When it is hot, strain the cream through a fine strainer to remove the flavouring ingredients. Pour the hot cream over the chocolate and set aside for 2 minutes. Stir until smooth, cool to 50°C (120°F). When the mixture is at the right temperature, blitz the butter in with a stick mixer until smooth. Allow the ganache to cool and become firm enough to pipe.

Assembling Macarons

Fill the piping bag with a 7 mm (³/8 in) plain nozzle with the ganache. Pipe the ganache onto the flat side of half a macaron shell, place another half macaroon shell onto the ganache and there you have it—a colourful plate of macarons.

TIP

Don't let the fillings here restrict you. Macarons can be filled with jams, curds, butter creams, jellies or even the peanut caramel included in this book.

WARM PINEAPPLE, APPLE & GINGER PASTRIES

Serves 6

VANILLA ICING SUGAR

1 vanilla bean, split
    lengthwise
80 g (2½ oz) icing
    (confectioners') sugar

**PINEAPPLE, APPLE AND GINGER
    FILLING**

½ large pineapple, peeled
    and cored
1 green apple, peeled
100 g (3½ oz) light palm
    sugar, grated
15 g (½ oz) butter
2 5g (¾ oz) stem ginger,
    minced

PASTRY

1 sheet puff pastry, makes 9
    pastries
45 g (1½ oz) Pineapple,
    Apple and Ginger Filling,
    per pastry sheet
1 egg
20 ml (²/₃ fl oz) water

*Light buttery baked parcels of sweet pineapple
and earthy ginger. A lovely accompaniment to a
freshly brewed herbal tea. ~ Libby*

Vanilla Icing Sugar
Place the ingredients together in an airtight container.
Shake well and let sit overnight before using. Keep
stored away from any moisture.

Pineapple, Apple And Ginger Filling
Cut the pineapple and apple into 5 mm (¼ in) dices.
    Combine all the ingredients into a saucepan and
place over a low heat. Bring to a simmer and cook
for 30 minutes, or until all the liquid has evaporated.
Remove from heat and allow to cool down. Keep
stored in an airtight container in the refrigerator.

Pastry
Preheat the oven to 200°C (400°F). Line a baking tray
with baking paper. Remove a puff pastry sheet from
the freezer.
    In a small bowl, whisk together the egg and water.
    Using a round pastry cutter, 7½ cm (3 in) in diameter,
cut 9 circles out of the pastry. Place 1 teaspoon of the
pineapple filling mixture into the centre of each circle.
    Brush the entire outside edges of each pastry circle
with the egg wash mixture. Fold up the sides, forming
a semi-circle and pinch the pastry edges together.
    Place pastries onto the baking tray, brush over with
more egg wash and bake for 12–14 minutes, or until
puffed and golden brown.

treats
185

To Serve
Allow the pastries to sit for 5–10 minutes after removing from the oven, as the fillings will be very hot. Arrange on a plate, dust with the Vanilla Icing Sugar and serve.

CHILLI CHOCOLATE BROWNIE

Serves 8

CHILLI BROWNIE

225 g (8 oz) dark chocolate,
    broken into chunks
140 g (5 oz) unsalted butter
200 g (7 oz) caster
    (superfine) sugar
1 teaspoon (5 g) vanilla
    extract
½ teaspoon (2.5 g) ground
    star anise
¼ teaspoon medium heat
    chilli powder
45 g (1½ oz) pine nuts
1 punnet fresh raspberries
2 eggs
1 egg yolk
85 g (3 oz) plain (all-purpose)
    flour, sifted

TO SERVE

Dutch cocoa powder, for
    dusting

A spicy blend of chilli and chocolate makes these brownies a decadent companion to serve with an after-dinner coffee or a well-brewed pot of tea. ~ Nadine

Chilli Brownie

Preheat oven to 180°C (350°F). Line a 20 cm (7¾ in) square tray with baking paper.

In a heatproof bowl, place 200 g (7oz) of the chocolate and all the butter and melt over a pan of simmering water. Stir once, making sure the butter and chocolate have completely melted. Stir in sugar, vanilla, star anise, chilli powder, pine nuts, raspberries and the extra chocolate chunks. Mix well, then add the eggs and sifted flour.

Bake for 35 minutes then cool, cut into desired size pieces.

To Serve

Dust with Dutch cocoa powder. Serve with freshly brewed coffee or tea.

DARK CHOCOLATE & BANANA RUM BALLS

Serves 6

150 g (5 oz) dark chocolate, chopped
100 g (3½ oz) pure icing sugar (pure confectioners' sugar), sifted
80 g (2½ oz) banana, mashed
80 g (2½ oz) almond meal
15 ml (½ fl oz) cream
30 ml (1 fl oz) dark rum
50 g (1¾ oz) desiccated coconut

Pull on your turtleneck and lace up your platforms as it's time for a retro revival. However, this time around, these perennial party favourites are totally gluten-free. ~ Libby

Put the chocolate into a clean dry bowl and place over a saucepan of simmering water, making sure the water level is well below the base of the bowl.

Once the chocolate has melted, remove from the heat and stir through the sugar, mashed banana, almond meal, cream and rum. Mix well. Refrigerate the mixture until it is firm. Roll the mixture into 18 small balls and toss them through the desiccated coconut until they are well coated. Keep stored in an airtight container in the refrigerator for up to 5 days.

To Serve
Serve these rum balls straight from the refrigerator onto your serving platter. As it's almost impossible to stop at just one rum ball, allow 2–3 rum balls per person.

RASPBERRY, WHITE CHOCOLATE & MINT CHILLED PUDDINGS
with toasted rice dust

Serves 6

TOASTED RICE DUST

50 g (1¾ oz) jasmine rice

RASPBERRY, WHITE CHOCOLATE & MINT PUDDINGS

50 g (1¾ oz) rice flour
500 ml (16 fl oz) milk
120 ml (4 fl oz) cream
80 g (2½ oz) caster (superfine) sugar
30 g (1 oz) mint leaves
120 g (¼ lb) white chocolate, chopped
180 g (6 oz) fresh raspberries

TO SERVE

10 g (1/3 oz) icing (confectioners') sugar

Smooth, sweet white chocolate always manages to bring out the best from sour, fruity raspberry—they are a couple which naturally complement each other. ~ Libby

Toasted Rice Dust
Preheat the oven to 200°C (400°F). Spread the uncooked rice over a baking tray and toast in the oven for 20 minutes, or until golden. Remove from oven and allow rice to cool. Grind rice to dust in an electric spice grinder.

Raspberry, White Chocolate & Mint Puddings
Place the rice flour and 250 ml (8½ fl oz) of the milk into a bowl and whisk together.

Combine the cream, sugar and remaining 250 ml (8½ fl oz) of milk into a saucepan, over a medium heat and bring to a simmer. Remove from heat, add the mint and allow to cool. Blend well with an electric blender and strain the liquid to remove the mint.

Return the milk mixture to a medium heat and bring to a boil. Whisk in the flour and milk mixture and cook for another 4 minutes, until the mixture thickens. Remove from the heat and stir in the white chocolate pieces. Set aside to cool a little.

Using half of the raspberries, divide them evenly between six 100 ml (2¾ fl oz) espresso glasses. Spoon the cooled pudding mix into a piping bag and pipe the mixture into the glasses. Place them in the refrigerator to chill for at least 30 minutes.

To Serve
Remove the puddings from the refrigerator. Sprinkle a layer of the Toasted Rice Dust across the top of each pudding. Scatter remaining raspberries evenly across puddings and dust with icing sugar.

JASMINE TEA CHOCOLATE TRUFFLES

Makes about 25

250 ml (8½ fl oz) pouring
    cream
20 g (²/₃ oz) jasmine tea
    leaves
600 g (21 oz) dark chocolate,
    finely chopped
Dutch cocoa powder, for
    dusting

A more-ish sweet finish to enjoy with after-dinner coffee. ~ Nadine

Bring cream and tea just to the boil over medium heat. Let stand for 20 minutes. Strain through a fine sieve.

Melt half the chocolate in a heatproof bowl over a saucepan of simmering water.

Remove from the heat, add cream mixture stirring well. Cover and refrigerate until set.

Melt 200 g of remaining chocolate over simmering water then add the last 100 g of chocolate, stirring until smooth.

Scoop balls of chocolate cream ganache using a melon baller, then dip each ball into the melted chocolate. Or, as in the photo, pipe the mixture into cigars, let chill, then dip into the melted chocolate.

Set aside onto wire rack and set. Dust each ball with Dutch cocoa powder. Can be kept in an airtight container for a week in the refrigerator.

KAFFIR LIME, WHITE CHOCOLATE & COCONUT TRUFFLES

Makes 24

½ cup (4 fl oz) thickened
    cream
4 kaffir lime leaves, leave 2
    whole and finely chop the
    other 2
250 g (9 oz) good-quality
    white chocolate, chopped
2 teaspoons (10 g) lime zest
130 g (4 oz) desiccated
    coconut

Coconut, lime and white chocolate are a beautiful combination. Orange or lemon can be substituted for the lime if you wish. ~ Nadine

Bring cream and the kaffir lime leaves to the boil, stirring continuously. Remove pan from the heat, take out the two whole kaffir lime leaves and add chopped chocolate. Let stand until cool (about ½ hour) and then beat with an electric mixer until light and smooth.

Blend in lime zest and ½ cup (45 g) coconut. Lightly toast the remaining 1 cup (85 g) of coconut in the oven.

Roll truffle mixture into balls or pipe into desired shapes, and roll in toasted coconut.

Keep refrigerated for up to 1 week.

CARAMELISED PEANUT & CHOCOLATE CLUSTERS

Makes 24

200 g (7 oz) caster (superfine)
    sugar
50 g (1¾ oz) butter
100 g (3 ½ oz) lightly
    toasted, unsalted
    peanuts
200 g (7 oz) dark chocolate

Small clusters of nuts set in luscious caramel then coated in dark chocolate. White or milk chocolate can also be used. ~ Nadine.

Line a baking tray with baking paper.

Melt the sugar in a heavy-based saucepan over very gentle heat. Once all the sugar has dissolved, stir in the butter.

Increase the heat and boil until it turns a mid-golden colour. Take off the heat.

Drop in a cluster of 3–4 nuts at a time, then scoop out at once with a metal spoon, placing cluster on the lined baking tray, repeat until all nuts have been used. Cool and set until firm.

Melt chocolate in a heatproof bowl over a double boiler. Dunk each cluster in the melted chocolate and place on lined tray.

Can be kept in an airtight container in the refrigerator for up to 3 days.

Photo clockwise from right:
Caramelised Peanut & Chocolate
Clusters, Kaffir Lime & Coconut
Truffles and Jasmine Tea
Chocolate Truffles.

SEA SALT & PISTACHIO CHOCOLATE FUDGE

Makes 36

50 g (¾ oz) butter, chopped
1 x 395g (14 oz) can
    condensed milk
1 teaspoon (5 g) vanilla
    extract
1 teaspoon (5 g) sea salt, plus
    a little extra for sprinkling
400 g (14 oz) dark chocolate,
    chopped
70 g (2½ oz) chopped
    pistachios
90 g (3 oz) crystallised ginger,
    diced

This recipe is quick and easy. Perfect for that after-school sweet treat. Can be kept in the refrigerator for a week—if they last that long. ~ Nadine

Place butter, condensed milk, vanilla and sea salt in a sauce pan and cook over medium heat, stirring until butter is melted.

Remove from the heat and add chopped chocolate, stir until melted and smooth.

Add the pistachios, ginger and stir to combine.

Pour into a baking paper-lined 20 cm (7¾ in) tin and smooth the surface with the back of a spoon.

Sprinkle with extra salt and refrigerate for 2 hours, then cut into squares.

LEMON, CLOVE, CINNAMON & SESAME SEED SWIRLS

Makes about 20 swirls

This recipe brings fond childhood memories of visits to Aunty Jose, who loved to make biscuits and cakes. Sweet spice baking aromas seemed to permanently waft through her house. ~ *Nadine*

BISCUIT DOUGH

300 g (10½ oz) self-raising (self-rising) flour
¼ teaspoon salt
1 teaspoon (15 g) caster (superfine) sugar
1 teaspoon (15 g) butter
1 egg
125 ml (4 fl oz) milk
1 extra egg for brushing

Biscuit Dough
Sift flour into a bowl. Add salt and sugar then rub in the butter.

Beat egg with the milk and add to the flour mix. Mix well to form dough. Roll out into a rectangle.

CINNAMON CLOVE APPLE FILLING

3 teaspoons (45 g) ground cinnamon
¼ teaspoon ground cloves
80 g (2½ oz) butter, softened
150 g (5 oz) brown sugar
1 green apple, finely sliced and peeled

Cinnamon Clove Apple Filling
Mix together cinnamon, cloves, softened butter and sugar.

Using a metal palette knife, spread the filling over the dough. Then place finely sliced apple on top of the filling leaving 1 cm (¾ in) around each edge. Roll dough up lengthwise, forming a long cylinder. Cut into 1 cm (¾ in) slices and place flat side up on a lined baking tray. Brush each lightly with beaten egg. Bake in oven at 180°C (350°F) for 15 minutes or until light golden brown.

LEMON ICING SUGAR

2 lemons, zested
100 g (3½ oz) icing (confectioners') sugar

Lemon Icing Sugar
Blanch lemon zest in boiling water for 2 minutes. Refresh in iced water and dry.

Put zest on a tray in very low oven at 50°C (122°F) for 20 minutes to thoroughly dry out. Blitz in coffee grinder until fine then mix into the icing sugar.

TO SERVE

10 g (⅓ oz) black sesame seeds

To Serve
While swirls are still warm, sprinkle them with the black sesame seeds, then dust swirls with the lemon icing sugar.

200

NUT, LIME & COCONUT CAKE
with lime syrup & whipped cream

Serves 6

This zesty moist cake gets extra bonus points for being so quick and easy to prepare. All the ingredients simply go straight into a food processor, then into the oven. Leaving you little to wash up and more time on your hands. ~ Libby

Whipped Cream
Refer to White Chocolate Meringue recipe.

Lime Syrup
125 g (4 oz) caster (superfine) sugar
125 ml (4 fl oz) water
100 ml (3½ fl oz) lime juice
1 lime, zest only

NUT, LIME & COCONUT CAKE
2 eggs
120 g (¼ lb) caster (superfine) sugar
50 g (1¾ oz) butter, soft
60 g (2 oz) macadamia or Brazil nuts, chopped finely
60 g (2 oz) desiccated coconut
1 lime, zest
125 ml (4 fl oz) lime juice
40 g (1½ oz) plain (all-purpose) flour
125 ml (4 fl oz) coconut cream

Whipped Cream
Refer to White Chocolate Meringue recipe.

Lime Syrup
Refer to Mango Panna Cotta with Lychee, Orange, Passionfruit Salad, Lime Syrup & Honey Wafer recipe.

Nut, Lime And Coconut Cake
Preheat your oven to 180°C (350°F). Line a 23 cm (9 in) × 13 cm (5 in) loaf tin with baking paper and non-stick spray. Place all ingredients together into an electric food processor and blitz for 30 seconds, or until the ingredients are well combined. Pour cake mix into a loaf tin and bake for 40 minutes, or until a skewer inserted into the cake centre comes out clean. Remove from the oven and allow to cool in the tin.

To Serve
With a warm knife that has been dipped into hot water and wiped dry, cut six serves from the cake. Any remaining cake can be served as second helpings or kept in an airtight container and refrigerated for 2 days. Place a dollop of Whipped Cream on top of each cake portion and drizzle the Lime Syrup over the cream and around the cake.

CINNAMON & CHILLI DUSTED DONUTS
with blood orange curd

Serves 6

CINNAMON AND CHILLI SUGAR
115 g (3¾ oz) caster
    (superfine) sugar
5 g (¼ oz) ground cinnamon
5 g (¼ oz) ground chilli
    powder

BLOOD ORANGE CURD
5 whole eggs
100 g (3½ oz) caster
    (superfine) sugar
125 ml (4 fl oz) blood orange
    juice
150 ml (5 fl oz) cream

DONUTS
70 g (3½ oz) butter
165 ml (5½ fl oz) water
100 g (3½ oz) plain (all-
    purpose) flour
pinch salt
2 whole eggs

Sweet, hot and spicy! These sugary hot donuts will remind you of childhood days, but the chilli hit will subtly bring you back to adult reality. Enjoy these with coffee, conversation and shared memories. ~ Libby

Cinnamon And Chilli Sugar
Combine all ingredients together. Add more ground chilli if you'd prefer a spicier mix.

Blood Orange Curd
Combine eggs, sugar and blood orange juice in a bowl. Whisk together until sugar dissolves. Pour in cream and mix well. Place bowl over a saucepan of simmering water, making sure water level is well below base of the bowl. Whisk continuously for around 12 minutes, until mixture is smooth and thick. This continuous stirring will prevent curd from having a grainy texture. Once all bubbles have disappeared from curd, the cooking is complete. Remove bowl from the heat. Allow curd to cool down, stirring occasionally. Set the curd in an airtight container in the refrigerator overnight. This curd can be kept refrigerated for up to 5 days.

Donuts
Place butter and water in a saucepan and bring to boil. Sift flour and salt together and with a wooden spoon stir into the boiling liquid. Once mixture is all well combined and coming away from the sides of the saucepan as you stir, remove from heat. Cover mix with cling film and set aside for 15 minutes.
    Transfer mix to an electric mixer and on a low speed,

add eggs, one at a time. Be sure to beat well between each egg.

Place dough into a piping bag fitted with a star-shaped nozzle and pipe out long lengths onto a tray. Place this tray into freezer and once dough is firm enough, cut into 6 cm (2¼ in) lengths. Pack down into airtight containers and keep in freezer until needed.

The dough can keep in freezer for up to 2 months.

To Serve

Half-fill a large wok with cooking oil and place over medium heat. Once the temperature has reached 180°C (350°F), the donuts are ready to be fried. Remove donuts straight from the freezer and fry in batches of six at a time so you don't over-crowd the wok. Donuts will only take a few minutes to cook and are done when they've turned a lovely golden colour. Remember to turn them occasionally as they are frying so they cook evenly. Scoop them out of the hot wok using a slotted spoon and onto some paper towel to soak up any excess oil.

Straight away roll the hot donuts in the Cinnamon and Chilli Sugar. Spoon the Blood Orange Curd into small serving bowls which are deep enough to plunge the donuts into. Serve immediately with plenty of napkins on the side for sticky fingers.

COCONUT MARSHMALLOW
with kaffir lime sherbet

Serves 6

KAFFIR LIME SHERBET

30 g (1 oz) kaffir lime leaves
½ teaspoon bicarbonate of
    soda (baking soda)
½ teaspoon citric acid
25 g (¾ oz) icing
    (confectioners') sugar

COCONUT MARSHMALLOW

30 g (1 oz) icing
    (confectioners') sugar
120 ml (4 fl oz) water
200 g (7 oz) caster
    (superfine) sugar
160 g (5½ oz) light corn
    syrup
2 titanium gelatine sheets
    (see Glossary)
10 ml (1/3 fl oz) Malibu white
    coconut rum

This recipe comes courtesy of our head chef, Ben. He wanted to recreate his childhood favourite, Whizz Fizz, and we were all more than willing to be taste-testers. Here the sour kaffir lime sherbet balances the sweet pillows of coconut marshmallow. ~ Libby

Kaffir Lime Sherbet

Blend the kaffir lime leaves in an electric spice grinder until they are a fine powder.

Using a fine sieve, sift all the ingredients together into a bowl. Stir the ingredients until they are well combined.

Keep stored in an airtight container away from any moisture for 3 days.

Coconut Marshmallow

Line a 23 × 13 cm (9 x 5 in) loaf tin with baking paper. Dust the base of the tin thickly with 15 g (½ oz) of the icing sugar .

Put 60 ml (2 fl oz) of water, the sugar and corn syrup into a small saucepan. Place over a medium heat and bring to a slow boil.

Meanwhile, soften the gelatine sheets in cold water. Squeeze out the excess water from the gelatine and place the softened gelatine into an electric kitchen mixer bowl with the remaining 60 ml (2 fl oz) of water. Attach the whisk beater.

Once the boiling sugar syrup mixture reaches a temperature of 115°C (240°F) on a sugar thermometer, remove from the heat and pour slowly onto your gelatine. Have your mixer whisking on its lowest speed. Once all the sugar syrup is added, increase the mixer's whisking speed to its highest setting. Continue to whisk on high for 10 minutes, until the mixture has tripled in size.

Add the Malibu and whisk it in well for 1 minute.

Pour the marshmallow mix into your prepared loaf tin. Dust the remaining 15 g (½ oz) of icing sugar across the top of the marshmallow. Cover with cling film and store in a dry cool place for 12 hours as it sets.

To Serve
Portion the marshmallow with a long cook's knife that's been dipped in cold water. Arrange the cut portions onto a serving platter and dust across their tops with a thick coat of the Kaffir Lime Sherbet. Any remaining marshmallow pieces can keep for up to 4 days in an airtight container, away from any moisture.

CHILLED MANGO PUDDING
with passionfruit curd & star anise coconut crumb

Serves 8

This refreshing chilled fruit pudding is perfect for a leisurely, hot afternoon pick-me-up. ~ Libby

STAR ANISE COCONUT CRUMB
50 g (1¾ oz) Crunchy Candied Coconut (see recipe)

10 g (¹/3 oz) ground star anise

PASSIONFRUIT CURD
1 quantity Blood Orange Curd from Cinnamon & Chilli Donut recipe

125 ml (4 fl oz) strained passionfruit juice, instead of blood orange juice

MANGO PUDDING
60 ml (2 fl oz) water

80 g (2½ oz) caster (superfine) sugar

1 titanium gelatine sheet (see Glossasry)

300 ml (10½ fl oz) mango puree

125 ml (4 fl oz) coconut cream

Star Anise Coconut Crumb
Place the Crunchy Candied Coconut into a pestle and mortar and pound to a fine crumb. Mix through the star anise and store in an airtight container, away from moisture for 3 days.

Passionfruit Curd
Simply exchange the blood orange juice in the recipe with the same quantity of strained passionfruit juice.

Mango Pudding
Combine the water and sugar into a saucepan, place over a medium heat and bring to a simmer. Remove from heat.

Soften the gelatine sheets in cold water, then squeeze out the excess water and add them to the warm sugar syrup, stirring well until they are all dissolved.

Add the mango puree and coconut cream to the sugar syrup and blend well with an electric blender.

Strain mixture and pour into eight 100 ml (2¾ fl oz) espresso glasses, about two-thirds full. Transfer the puddings to the refrigerator to chill for at least 2 hours.

To Serve
Remove your mango puddings from the refrigerator. Fill the remaining third of each glass with the Passionfruit Curd. Sprinkle a fine layer of the Star Anise Coconut Crumb across the top of each glass.

BLING

CANDIED BANANA SLICES

Makes approximately 30 slices

500 ml (16 fl oz) vegetable oil for frying
2 bananas, peeled and finely sliced lengthways
225 g (8 oz) caster (superfine) sugar
250 ml (8½ fl oz) water

Use these crispy chips to garnish banana cake, ice cream or my White Chocolate & Chai Mousse. ~ Renee

In a heavy-based saucepan, heat oil to 160°C (325°F). Fry bananas until golden, they will get crispier as they cool.

Heat sugar and water in a saucepan until sugar is dissolved, then reduce to a syrup consistency. Take off heat.

Using a fork, dip banana slices in syrup, then lay on a tray lined with greaseproof paper to cool.

Bananas should be crispy. If not, place in a 100°C (200°F) oven for 20–30 minutes to dry further.

Store in an airtight container between pieces of greaseproof paper at room temperature. Will keep for about 3 to 5 days.

CANDIED RHUBARB

Makes enough to garnish 6
desserts

*A superfine, strikingly unusual garnish for just
about any dessert. ~ Nadine*

2 rhubarb stalks
100 g (3½ oz) icing
(confectioners') sugar

Preheat the oven to 50°C (122°F).

Peel the rhubarb with your hands, making long strips.

Place on a tray lined with baking paper and sprinkle
heavily with the icing sugar.

Leave in the oven for 1–2 hours until rhubarb feels
dry.

Store in an airtight container. Keeps for 2 weeks.

CARAMELISED BANANA SLICES

Makes enough to garnish 6
serves

2 bananas, ripe and firm
10 g (¹⁄3 oz) butter
60 g (2 oz) brown sugar

A simple garnish to dress up a chocolate pudding or even just a scoop of ice cream. ~ Libby

Slice the bananas, on an angle, into 7 mm (¼ in) thick pieces. Roll them into the brown sugar and press down to coat well. Heat a large frypan over medium heat. Add the butter and when it begins to bubble, add the banana pieces. Allow to cook for 1–2 minutes each side, or until caramelised. Remove from heat and serve while warm.

CHILLI CANDY

Makes enough candy to
garnish 6–8 desserts

250 ml (8½ fl oz) sugar syrup,
made from 125 ml (4 fl
oz) water and 125 g (4 oz)
sugar brought to the boil
4 long red chillies, deseeded
and pith removed

*These fine strips of sweet peppery chilli add a
dash of crimson to brighten any dish. ~ Nadine*

Very thinly julienne the chillies and pat dry.

Bring the sugar syrup to the boil and drop in chilli
strips for about 3–4 minutes.

Remove from the heat and place chillies on tray
lined with baking paper to dry out.

Can be stored in the refrigerator in dry airtight
container for up to 2 weeks.

CRUNCHY CANDIED COCONUT

Makes enough to garnish 10 serves

100 g (3½ oz) coconut, zested
50 g (1¾ oz) sugar
40 ml (1½ fl oz) water
pinch salt

What a versatile garnish! These crisp, curly, lovely long strands of golden toasted coconut flesh will bring a sweet nutty crunch to any dessert. Use them to garnish my Dark Chocolate and Star Anise Rice Puddings, Ginger and Coconut Tapioca Pudding or Pumpkin Crème Caramels.
~ Libby

To zest the coconut, crack a coconut in half using a solid blunt instrument. A pestle will work really well. To do this, simply lay the coconut sideways in the palm of one hand and firmly tap down on its widest point with the other. Whilst tapping, rotate the coconut away from you like you are following a line around its centre. When the coconut cracks open, be aware the coconut water will spray out. (This water is not needed for this recipe, however if you collect, strain and chill it all, you will have a most refreshing drink.)

Lay a coconut half on your chopping board. With the cracked edge at right angles with your board, use a hand-held zester to zest long strands of the fresh coconut flesh.

Place the sugar, water and salt into a saucepan over medium heat. Once the sugar has dissolved, add the coconut zest and stir until all the liquid has evaporated. Turn the coconut out onto an oven tray and bake at 180°C (350°F) for 15 minutes, or until golden brown and crisp. Allow to cool on the tray. Pack into an airtight container and store away from any moisture, for up to 1 week.

RASPBERRY DUST

Makes enough to garnish 10
serves

175 g (6 oz) raspberries
15 g (½ oz) icing
(confectioners') sugar

This powder adds an intensely floral perfume, a big fruity sweet-and-sour flavour and a gorgeous pink hue. Sprinkle across my Frozen Dark Chocolate, Raspberry, Chilli Mousse Cake or the Raspberry, White Chocolate and Mint Chilled Rice Puddings or the Poached Peaches. ~ Libby

Quarter the raspberries and place them spread out on a lined baking tray. Sift an even layer of icing sugar over the raspberries. Dry them out in your oven set on its lowest temperature for at least 6 hours.

Once completely dried, blitz them to a rough powder in an electric spice grinder. Keep in an airtight container, away from any moisture, for 1 month.

CANDIED GINGER CHIPS

Makes enough candy to
garnish 6 desserts

20 g (²/3 oz) ginger, peeled
100 g (3½ oz) caster
    (superfine) sugar
100 ml (2¾ fl oz) water

Small sweet ginger chips that pack a deceivingly big kick of heat. Scatter sparingly across Ginger and Tapioca puddings, White Chocolate, Ginger and Pistachio Meringues, Mango Panna Cotta or Poached Peaches. ~ Libby

Preheat the oven to its lowest setting and line an oven tray with baking paper.

Thinly slice the ginger diagonally across its fibres.

Place the sugar and water into a saucepan over a medium heat and bring to a simmer. Once the sugar has dissolved, place ginger slices into the syrup and stir until well coated.

Remove from heat and strain ginger out of the syrup. You can reserve the syrup and use it to drizzle over any dessert for a hint of sweet ginger. It will keep in the refrigerator for up to one month.

Using two forks, spread the individual ginger slices out flat, spaced apart across the oven tray. Place the tray in oven and allow to dry overnight.

Store candied ginger chips in an airtight container, away from moisture for up to 1 month.

LEMON CANDY

Makes enough candy to
garnish 6 desserts

1 lemon, zest and all pith
removed
125 ml (4 fl oz) water
125 g (4 oz) sugar

*A delicate garnish with a tang for the
Deconstructed Citrus Tart. ~ Nadine*

Finely slice the zest of the lemon.
  Blanch the lemon zest in boiling water for 2 minutes.
Pat dry.
  Make some sugar syrup by bringing the water and the
sugar to a boil in a saucepan, over a medium heat.
  Drop lemon zest into syrup, bring back to the boil for
3 minutes.
  Remove from the heat and cool. Store in refrigerator
for up to a month in the syrup.

SALTED PEANUT CARAMEL

Makes 1 litre (36 fl oz)

300 ml (10½ fl oz) cream
120 g (4 oz) glucose syrup
180 g (6 oz) caster
    (superfine) sugar
80 g (2½ oz) butter, diced
140 g (5 oz) salted peanuts,
    roughly chopped
pinch salt

Here a delicious sweet and creamy caramel has its flavour enhanced with salted crunchy peanuts. Spoon it over my Banana Bavarois, or serve simply over scoops of vanilla and chocolate ice cream with a drizzle of Chocolate Vanilla Sauce.
~ Libby

Combine the cream and glucose syrup into a small saucepan and bring to a slow boil over a low heat.

At the same time, place a heavy-based saucepan over medium heat and add one tablespoon of the sugar. Once the saucepan is warm enough to melt the sugar, sprinkle in the remaining sugar. Stir constantly until all sugar has melted and is a light brown colour. Ss soon as the caramel begins to darken and slightly smoke, pour over boiled cream mix. Be aware that the mixture will now bubble and spit up. Stir the mix until the caramel is lump free.

Remove from heat and whisk in diced butter. Once fully incorporated, stir through peanuts and salt. Cool to room temperature and store in an airtight container, away from any moisture, for up to one week.

TURMERIC SUGAR

Makes 12 discs

200 g (7 oz) iso-malt (see Glossary)
20 ml (²/₃ fl oz) water
20 g (²/₃ oz) fresh turmeric, peeled and pounded in a mortar

An absolutely stunning and vibrant sugar garnish.
~ Nadine

Preheat oven to 180°C (350°F).

Place iso-malt and water into pan on low heat until the iso-malt has dissolved.

Peel, chop and pound the turmeric in a mortar and pestle. Place turmeric in a clean dishcloth and squeeze out the liquid into a separate bowl. Add turmeric liquid, drop by drop, into the iso-malt until the desired colour is achieved. Pour liquid onto the lined tray and set aside. Once cool, break up sugar and blend in a coffee or spice grinder. Grind until it is a fine powder.

On another lined tray, place 6 teaspoons of powder onto the tray, like cookies. Each teaspoon will make one disc. Make sure each teaspoonful is evenly spaced, as in the photo opposite.

Place into the oven for 5 minutes, then check. The discs should be bubbly. If not, leave for a little while longer. Remove from oven and let cool slightly, then peel off the tray and mould sugar into desired shapes.

Both the powder and cooked disks can be kept in an airtight container in the freezer for up to 3 weeks.

SUGAR GARNISHES

Serves 6

120 g (4 oz) caster
  (superfine) sugar
60 ml (2 fl oz) water
80 g (2½ oz) glucose syrup
  (see Glossary)

These crisp caramel garnishes give desserts, cakes or cocktails an attractive decorative finish. Here you are the designer, so let loose your inner artist. Adding a few drops of food dye to the syrup can expand your creativity. ~ Libby

Line an oven tray with baking paper.

Place the sugar and water into a small heavy-based saucepan, carefully stirring the mixture to lift the sugar off the bottom. Bring to a boil over a medium heat. Once boiling, add the glucose and allow the mix to return to the boil.

Half-fill a bowl, one larger than the size of your saucepan, with ice and cold water.

Keep a careful eye on the sugar syrup as it is boiling to watch for a gradual change in colour. Once it has reached a light amber colour, remove the saucepan from the heat and dip its bottom straight into the prepared iced water bath for 5 seconds; this will stop the cooking process.

Dip the handle end of a long wooden spoon into the hot syrup. The syrup is ready to be worked with when, as the spoon is drawn out of the syrup, it holds a long continuous stream.

Twirl the syrup off the end of the spoon onto your lined oven tray, to create your sugar garnishes. As it is all freehand, you can make any shapes you desire.

Should your sugar syrup cool down and become too thick before you've finished, simply place the saucepan over a low heat to soften the syrup.

Once the garnishes have set hard, store them between layers of baking paper in an airtight container in the freezer for up to 2 months. Serve these sugar garnishes straight from the freezer.

CANDIED SWEET POTATO

Makes 12–15 pieces

100 g (3½ oz) caster
    (superfine) sugar
150 ml (5 fl oz) water
12–15 thin strips of peeled
    sweet potato (kumara)

A crunchy garnish to serve with Sweet Potato &
Ginger Pudding. ~ Renee

Preheat the oven to 100°C (200°F).

Place sugar and water in a saucepan, dissolve sugar then reduce to a syrup.

While syrup is simmering, add sweet potato strips and cook for 3–4 minutes.

Remove sweet potato and place on a tray lined with greaseproof paper. Discard syrup.

Place sweet potato in oven and cook for 30 minutes or until potato dries and becomes crispy.

Store in an airtight container until required.

CHOCOLATE SHARDS

100 g (3½ oz) good-quality
cooking chocolate

These jagged shards add a dash of chocolate
drama to so many different desserts. ~ Nadine

Place chocolate in a bowl over a pot of simmering water.

Stir occasionally until smooth. Do not let the bottom of the bowl touch the water.

Cut 2 sheets of 40 x 30 cm (16 x 12 in) non-stick baking paper.

Pour melted chocolate onto one of the sheets, spread the chocolate with a spatula until a thin even layer has formed, leave about 2 cm (¾ in) each side.

Place second sheet on top of the chocolate and smooth out with a ruler.

Roll up from the short end making a tube, refrigerate for 2 hours or until set.

Hold end of papers and unroll, the chocolate will break into shards. Take off top sheet.

Store shards in a flat airtight container lined with baking paper for up to 2 weeks.

CHOCOLATE CURLS

400 g (14 oz) dark chocolate, chopped

These attractive chocolate curls can decorate all sorts of desserts and can be made days ahead of time. ~ Libby

Line a 23 × 13 cm (9 x 5 in) loaf tin with baking paper.

Put the chocolate into a clean dry bowl and place over a saucepan of simmering water, making sure the water level is well below the base of the chocolate bowl. Once the chocolate has all melted, give it a good stir and pour it into the lined container.

Allow the chocolate to cool down to room temperature.

Using the baking paper, lift the chocolate out of the loaf tin and lay it flat on a folded tea towel on your bench. Using a small round pastry cutter 5 cm (2 in) in diameter, hold on a slight angle so the far side of the cutter is touching the chocolate surface and scrape the cutter towards yourself. The chocolate will naturally curl up into the centre of the cutter.

Keep these chocolate curls in an airtight container in your refrigerator for up to 7 days.

CHOCOLATE BRANDY SNAP

Makes approximately 20 snaps

225 g (8 oz) caster (superfine) sugar
125g (4 oz) unsalted butter
4 tablespoons (60 g) glucose syrup
100 g (3½ oz) plain (all-purpose) flour
25g (¾ oz) cocoa powder

Serve with Chocolate Rum Ice Cream or as a garnish for the Chocolate Brûlée with Raspberry Chilli Jam. ~ Nadine

Preheat oven to 160°C (325°F).

Melt sugar, butter and glucose in a saucepan over low heat, do not colour. Take off the heat and add sifted flour and cocoa powder.

Roll into logs about ¾ in (2 cm) in diameter, refrigerate until firm. Cut thin slices and place onto baking tray, six at a time. Cook for about 8 minutes until mixture bubbles. Remove from oven and curl around the end of a wooden spoon.

Store in refrigerator in airtight container lined with baking paper for up to 1 week.

SESAME TUILE

Makes 12

1 tablespoon sesame seeds
50 g (1¾ oz) butter
50 g (1¾ oz) caster
    (superfine) sugar
1 vanilla bean
50 g (1¾ oz) plain (all-
    purpose) flour
2 egg whites

Use tuiles to decorate creamy desserts, like Coconut Rice Mousse, Spiced Ice Cream or my Coconut Passionfruit Brûlée. ~ Renee

In a dry pan over a medium heat, toast sesame seeds until golden, then set aside to cool until needed.

Cream together butter and sugar until well combined.

Split vanilla bean down the middle and scrap out seeds, add seeds to butter and sugar.

Sift flour and add to mix, and then add toasted sesame seeds.

Whisk egg whites until soft peaks are forming. One-third at a time, fold the egg whites into mix. Let the mix rest for at least 30 minutes in refrigerator until needed.

Cut a rectangle out of the middle of the lid of an old plastic container to use as a template.

Preheat oven to 160°C (325°F).

Line a tray with greaseproof paper and, using the template, spread a thin, even layer of tuile mix. Remove template, repeat. Cook in oven for 8–10 minutes or until sides are golden.

As soon as you remove tuile from oven, wrap around a large round object (wooden spoon handle is ideal). Leave for 5 seconds then remove. The tuile will become crisp on cooling and will stay curled.

It's best to cook tuiles in batches of two as you don't want the tuiles to crisp up before you can curl them. Continue for six batches or until you have 12 tuiles. Once the tuiles are cooled keep them an airtight container; they will last for about 3 to 5 days.

PINEAPPLE WAFER SWIZZLE STICKS

Makes approximately 12 sticks

75 g (2½ oz) butter
125 g (½ cup) pineapple diced
50 g (1¾ oz) plain (all-purpose) flour
200 g (6½ oz) pure icing (confectioners') sugar

A crispy garnish for my Mango Passionfruit Parfait or use as a 'dipper biscuit' with Passionfruit Cream. ~ Nadine.

Place all ingredients in a blender, process until smooth. Line a baking tray with baking paper.

Place ½ teaspoonfuls of batter on the tray, each spread out to a thin circle about 10 cm (4 in) in diameter.

Cook in 160°C (325°F) oven for 5–10 minutes or until just starting to turn golden.

When cooked, use a spatula to lift off the baking paper and roll each biscuit around a pencil to form a swizzle stick. Let cool.

If the biscuits cool before you have rolled them, just place them back in the oven for a couple of seconds—but don't burn them!

Once they have cooled keep in an airtight container in the refrigerator until needed. Will last 3 to 5 days.

CRISP HONEY WAFERS

Makes 24 wafers

30 g (1 oz) butter, melted
15 g (½ oz) honey
1 egg white
45 g (1½ oz) icing
   (confectioners') sugar,
   sifted
40 g (1½ oz) plain (all-
   purpose) flour, sifted

These light dainty wafers add a little crunch to soft desserts such as my Mango Panna Cotta, Chilled Mango Puddings with Passionfruit Curd and Raspberry, White Chocolate and Mint Chilled Rice Puddings. ~ Libby

In an electric mixer beat the melted butter and honey until smooth. Beat in the egg white, then the sifted sugar and flour. Mix until well combined then cover and set aside for 1 hour.

Heat oven to 170°C (340° F) and line an oven tray with baking paper. Drop one teaspoon of the wafer batter onto the tray. Repeat this six times, spacing across the whole tray. Using the back of the teaspoon, smear the batter into thin 5 cm (2 in) rounds. The batter won't smear evenly, that's fine. Bake for 5–7 minutes, or until golden. Remove from oven and while still warm, lift them with a flat spatula and drape over a rolling pin to curl. Should the wafers cool down and become too firm to be curled, simply return them to the oven for 1 minute. Repeat this process until you have the amount of wafers you need. This recipe yields 24 cooked wafers; however, any unused wafer mix can be stored in an airtight container in your refrigerator for up to 1 week. Store cooked wafers in an airtight container, away from moisture, for 2 days.

PISTACHIO NUT PRALINE

Makes 20 serves

120 g (4 oz) pistachio nuts,
    shelled
250 g (8½ oz) caster
    (superfine) sugar
100 ml (2¾ fl oz) water

With its flecks of green nut and golden toffee, this praline adds a crunch and colour to my White Chocolate, Ginger Pistachio Meringues. It can be served broken into large shards, roughly chopped, or blitzed into a fine powder. You can swap the pistachios for any other nut of your choice. ~ Libby

Preheat the oven to 180°C (350°F).

Lightly toast the pistachio nuts for 3–5 minutes on a tray lined with baking paper in the oven. Allow the nuts to cool on the tray.

Place the sugar and water into a heavy-based saucepan and lightly stir to remove the sugar from the base. Place over a medium heat and bring to the boil. While boiling, the mix will start to turn a light caramel. Swirl the saucepan as the colour increases. Remove from heat when colour has reached a lovely golden amber colour and pour straight over the toasted pistachio nuts.

Allow the praline to cool to room temperature and pack down into airtight containers. Keep stored in your freezer for up to 2 months

PEANUT PRALINE

200 g (7 oz) unsalted
peanuts
200 g (7 oz) granulated
sugar
15 ml (½ fl oz) water

Crumble over my Passionfruit Marshmallows—a taste bliss combination. ~ Nadine

Roast peanuts in 160°C (320°F) oven for 5–10 minutes and keep warm.

Put sugar and water in small saucepan and melt over a medium heat.

When the sugar starts to turn an amber colour, add the peanuts, making sure all nuts are coated with the sugar.

Pour onto a tray lined with baking paper. Wait until the toffee completely cools, then store in an airtight container in the freezer. Keeps for one month.

CHOCOLATE PISTACHIO PRALINE

40 g (1½ oz) shelled
 pistachio nuts
pinch salt
160 g (5½ oz) caster
 (superfine) sugar
50 ml (1¾ fl oz) water
50 g (1¾ oz) dark chocolate

Adds a nutty chocolate crunch, especially to any chocolate desserts. Use to garnish my Chocolate, Orange & Star Anise Parfait. ~ Renee

In a dry pan, toast pistachio nuts until golden and fragrant, then roughly chop.

Line a medium tray with baking paper, scatter pistachio nuts around then sprinkle with a pinch of salt.

In a clean saucepan, place sugar and water over a medium heat, dissolve sugar without stirring. Gently shake pan to help combine.

Continue cooking until sugar syrup turns golden. If sugar crystals form around edges, carefully brush with extra water using a pastry brush. When sugar syrup is a rich golden colour, carefully pour over nuts on tray and allow to cool.

When sugar has cooled, it should be hard like toffee. Using a mortar and pestle, smash the praline until there are no whole nuts or large pieces of toffee. Store in an airtight container in freezer.

Roughly chop chocolate until it is in very small pieces. When praline is cold, add chocolate and stir through the praline mix. Return to freezer until needed.

COCKTAILS

LEMONGRASS BASE SYRUP

8 stalks lemongrass
2 cups white sugar
8 cups water

The common base to many Spirit House cocktails is this fragrant lemongrass syrup. Make a batch and keep refrigerated for up to 2 weeks.

Bruise and chop lemongrass roughly, place in saucepan with sugar and water.
Bring to the boil, simmer for 2 hours.
Cool then strain into clean 2 litre (70 fl oz) container.

LOCO COCO

60 ml (2 fl oz) coconut rum
20 ml (²/3fl oz) lemongrass
   syrup
30 ml (1 fl oz) fresh lime

Dream of a beach fringed with gently swaying coconut palms? One lick of Loco Coco and you're almost there. Serve in an old-fashioned tumbler glass.

Combine ingredients in an iced shaker and shake vigorously.
Strain into iced glass and garnish with single orchid (make sure the orchid is washed).

LOTUS MOON

30 ml (1 fl oz) vodka
30 ml (1 fl oz) lemongrass
    syrup
3 chunks lime
4 torn mint leaves
sparkling pink grapefruit soft
    drink

Take one dainty sip and greet the rising moon with a smile. Serve in a short hurricane glass.

Muddle all ingredients except for grapefruit lightly in a short hurricane glass.
   Add ice and top with sparkling pink grapefruit. Garnish with a lemongrass stalk.

SPICED PEAR BELLINI

white sugar
ground five spice
30 ml (1 fl oz) pear nectar
Prosecco sparkling wine

The perfect palate wake-up call—bubbles, exotic spices and heavenly nectar. Easy to make, even easier to drink. Serve in a champagne flute.

Rim a chilled champagne flute with sugar mixed with five spice powder, add pear nectar then slowly add sparkling wine, stirring to combine ingredients.

MELLOW MELON

handful watermelon pieces
scoop of ice
5–6 mint leaves, shredded
30 ml (1 fl oz) lemongrass
    syrup
30 ml (1 fl oz) apple juice
60 ml (2 fl oz) cranberry juice

A tangy, fruit, non-alcoholic mock-tail to quench the thirst after a long hot day. Serve in short hurricane glass.

Place all ingredients in a blender, blend and serve.

THAI ICED TEA

15 ml (½ fl oz) each of
    Bacardi, Cointreau,
    Vodka, Gin
30 ml (1 fl oz) ginger syrup
30 ml (1 fl oz) lime juice
splash cola
6 lime chunks
6 fresh ginger chunks
2 slices lemon
iced lemon tea cubes (see
    below)

An Asian twist on this classic tea cocktail. Serve in a tall hurricane glass.

Muddle the ingredients in shaker with chunks of lime and fresh ginger chunks.
   Add ice and shake well. Pour contents into glass, add 2 slices of lemon.
   Top with iced tea cubes and a splash of coke.

Lemon Tea Ice cubes
Stir together 8 heaped teaspoons of lemon-flavoured ice tea powder and 1 litre (36 fl oz) of water. Pour into ice cube trays and freeze.

GINGER FIZZ

30 ml (1 fl oz) lemongrass
   syrup
3 chunks of lime
4 mint leaves shredded
ginger beer

Light, refreshing and non-alcoholic … for the long-suffering, designated driver. Serve in a long, narrow glass.

Muddle the ingredients in a tall hurricane glass, half-fill with ice, top up with ginger beer.

HOT BANGKOK

4 pieces watermelon
30 ml (1 fl oz) chilli infused
   vodka
10 ml (1/3 fl oz) lime juice
10 ml (1/3 fl oz) lemon grass
   syrup
60 ml (2 fl oz) mango nectar

Essential flavours of Thai cuisine—sweet, sour, hot—all muddled together in a short glass.

Muddle all ingredients in a shaker, strain and pour into a short glass with ice.
   Garnish with thin slice of red chilli.

PHUKET SUNSET

3 pieces of lime
6 pieces of ginger
60 ml (2 fl oz) vodka
50 ml (1¾ fl oz) apple juice
50 ml (1¾ fl oz) cranberry
  juice
10 ml (¹/₃ fl oz) ginger syrup
pickled ginger, to garnish

A cooling finish to a day on the beach—or a great start to a summer party. Serve in a highball glass.

Muddle lime and ginger in a shaker, add all other ingredients and shake well, strain and serve over ice. Garnish with pickled ginger.

LONG ISLAND ICED TEA

15 ml (½ fl oz) each of
  Bacardi, Cointreau,
  Vodka, Gin
30 ml (1 fl oz) lemongrass
  syrup
30 ml (1 fl oz) lime juice
fresh lime, chopped into
  chunks
fresh ginger, peeled,
  chopped into small
  chunks
2 slices lemon
iced tea cubes (recipe in
  Thai Iced Tea cocktail)
splash of cola

Cleansing citrus, a hint of fragrant ginger, a splash of cola. So enticing … even without the alcohol! Serve in a tall hurricane glass.

Muddle the ingredients in a shaker with six chunks of lime and fresh ginger chunks. Add small amount of ice and shake well. Pour contents into glass, add lemon slices. Top with iced tea cubes and a dash of cola.

GLOSSARY

Almond meal
Almond meal is blanched almonds ground down to a flour-like consistency. Almond meal adds a rich nutty taste and moisture to baked pastries and cakes, and is gluten-free and low in carbohydrates. In France, almond meal is called 'frangipane'.

Asian basil seeds
Also known as Thai or Oriental Basil, this basil has a strong licorice or anise flavour. The leaves, flowers and seeds are all eaten. Soak the seeds in a little water and they will become gelatinous—and look similar to dragon fruit seed. When drizzled over ice cream, sorbets or desserts, the seeds add texture and form an unusual garnish.

Baking paper
These cellulose-based papers have a non-stick coating which is able to withstand high oven temperatures. The paper eliminates the need to grease cake tins and baking trays.

Beating egg whites
Beating egg whites to the correct stage for a recipe is very important. It's best to keep watch when beating egg whites to ensure they do not become over-beaten.

Soft peak stage: means when the beater is lifted, the egg whites should just hold their shape.

Firm peak stage: means that the eggs hold their shape firmly when the beater is lifted.

Bicarbonate of soda (Baking soda)
This raising agent contains bicarbonate of soda (baking soda) plus an acid such as cream of tartar and a moisture-absorbing agent such as cornflour (cornstarch). It is a dual-action leavening agent because when mixed with liquid, as well as when exposed to dry heat, it releases carbon dioxide gas bubbles which cause the baking item to rise.

Brown sugar
Brown sugar is refined white sugar that has been coated with a film of molasses. The molasses is a viscous by-product in the refining process of the sugar and imparts a rich deep flavour and colour.

Cardamom
Cardamom is a member of the ginger family and green cardamom seeds are found inside highly aromatic papery pods. The pods are opened and discarded and only the small seeds are ground. Cardamom offers a warm fragrant eucalyptus aroma with lemony undertones. Highly aromatic, use sparingly. It adds a delicacy and freshness to desserts. This spice is used in two ways. The dark brown oily seeds inside the green papery pods are removed and ground, or the whole pod is lightly bruised and added to infuse flavour before being discarded.

Caster (superfine) sugar/Granulated sugar
A superfine white sugar, caster sugar dissolves easily and fast, so is ideal for meringues or cakes mixes. When baked, the super fine sugar crystals caramelise evenly, producing a fine golden colour.

Chai Syrup
Chai is simply the word for 'tea' in many Asian languages. Chai syrup is based on the Indian *masala chai,* a milky, sweetened spiced tea predominantly flavoured with ginger, cardamon, cinnamon and cloves. The syrup contains tea, natural spice flavours, sugar cane and water. Available only from gourmet food stores.

Chocolate—White vs Dark

Dark chocolate is made from the ground cocoa bean, so contains cocoa bean powder, cocoa butter, sugar, but no added milk solids. White chocolate contains sugar, cocoa butter and milk solids but no cocoa bean powder, so does not really taste like chocolate since it has no cocoa.

Cinnamon

Cinnamon quills consist of many layers of paper-thin pieces of aromatic bark tightly rolled up together. This earthy spice brings a fragrant, sweet and delicate flavour to desserts. Cinnamon is used in two ways, either as whole quills, which infuse their flavour, or as finely ground cinnamon powder.

Citric Acid

Citric acid is naturally found in many fruits, particularly citrus, as well as vegetables and is produced by many living organisms, including mould. Its sour flavour creates a refreshingly tart taste and balances out sweetness. Its acidic pH makes it very useful as a preservative in jams as many bacteria are unable to grow in its acid environment.

Cocoa Powder

Cocoa powder is what remains once 75 per cent of the cocoa butter from the cocoa solids in chocolate liquor is removed. The two main types available are Natural and Dutch-processed. Natural cocoa is bitter and mildly acidic. Dutch cocoa is alkalised to remove the natural acidity, reduce its bitterness and enhance its colour and flavour. Due to the differences between the two cocoa powders do not substitute one for the other in recipes.

Coconut Cream (Kara Brand)

Coconut cream is made by a process of squeezing heated water through fresh coconut. This very thick, creamy and enriching product is essentially a highly concentrated form of coconut milk.

With the Kara brand of UHT coconut products, the cream is milled from fresh coconut flesh into a creamy white paste, making it ideal for puddings, ice creams or desserts.

Condensed Milk

Wonderful for making caramel, condensed milk is simply cow's milk with the water removed and sugar added.

Cornflour (Cornstarch)

A fine gluten-free white powder milled from corn and used as a thickening agent.

Corn Syrup (see Glucose Syrup)

Couverture Chocolate

Dark, milk and white couverture chocolate all have a cocoa butter content of at least 32 per cent. This gives the chocolate a rich intense flavour, high sheen and luscious texture, perfect for high-quality desserts. Store your couverture chocolate covered at a temperature below 18°C (64°F). Avoid using any chocolate sold as a compound.

Care is required when melting chocolate. The chocolate should first be chopped or grated, then melted, preferably over a double boiler. Always use a low temperature and watch that no water comes in contact with the chocolate or it will seize up and form a thick grainy mass. Only use direct heat if the chocolate is in combination with cream or butter. Chocolate can be melted in the microwave—don't cover the bowl—microwave on medium for 1–2 minutes.

Cream—Pure, Whipping, Double etc

The types of cream vary widely in both names and fat content. Cream can be divided into the following milk fat per cent groups:

18–25% milk fat: a reduced fat cream for pouring.

35% milk fat with added gelatine: a good cream for both pouring and whipping.

35–45% milk fat: a good cream for heating and whipping.

48–55% milk fat: a thick, rich double cream for accompanying desserts.

Crystallised Ginger

Made from small cubes of ginger root simmered in sugar and water, then tossed with more sugar until the ginger is coated, then dried.

Cumquat

Symbolising good luck in China and Asia, these small citrus fruits are about the size of a large olive. The rind is incredibly sweet but the juicy flesh has a sour lemon taste. Cumquats are processed into preserves, jams, marmalades and pickles and are a delicious accompaniment to rich meats like duck or pork.

Dutch Cocoa (see Cocoa Powder)

Gelatine (see Leaf Gelatine)

Ginger

Ginger is an essential fresh ingredient in so many Asian recipes. Very young rhizomes, known as stem ginger or green ginger, are peeled and eaten raw in salads, added to stir fry, curries, pickled or cooked in syrup to make candied ginger for desserts.

Don't buy ginger rhizomes if the skin is dark and withered. Choose firm-skinned pieces and peel them thinly, as the flesh nearest the skin has the most flavour. The easiest way to peel ginger is to scrape the skin off with the edge of a soup spoon. Store peeled, sliced ginger in a plastic bag in the freezer or will keep for 3–4 weeks in an airtight container in the refrigerator.

Glucose Syrup (also known as Liquid Glucose or Corn Syrup)

Often called corn syrup, this clear sweet syrup is made from the hydrolysis of various starch crops including potatoes, wheat, barley, corn, rice and cassava. Due to being highly processed and purified in its making, tests have found very little, if any, residual gluten in this sometimes wheat-based product. It has the same uses as light cornstarch and the two can be easily exchanged in any recipe. With a strong sugar flavour and a very low freezing point, the syrup is ideal for ice creams and candy. It helps to preserve food, does not crystallise and is also a good preservative.

Gluten

Gluten is a protein found commonly in wheat and related grain species, including barley and rye. It is used as a food additive in the form of a flavour enhancer, a thickener and a stabiliser. Gluten-free labelling on a product indicates it contains less than the minimum standard that is considered to be harmful to someone with a gluten allergy.

Golden Syrup

A beautiful amber-coloured treacle, golden syrup is processed from sugar cane or sugar beet. The high fructose content gives it a sweeter taste than the equivalent quantity of white sugar, while its moisture and colour make golden syrup a great baking ingredient for cakes, puddings and biscuits. It is an ideal substitute for honey, particularly for vegans.

Granulated Sugar

Granulated sugar is white refined sugar, made by dissolving and purifying raw sugar then drying it to prevent clumping. It comes in a variety of crystal sizes including coarse-grained (such as decorating sugar), normal table sugar, fine-grade caster sugar and powdered icing sugar.

Hard Ball/Soft Ball Sugar Syrup

There are several stages that sugar goes through when heated. These include the thread, soft ball, hard ball, soft and hard crack stages.

Soft Ball: when the sugar syrup reaches 120°C (248°F), the liquid will be syrupy and the bubbles enlarge. Drop a teaspoonful of this syrup into a glass of icy water—if it forms a soft ball, it is ready.

Hard Ball: this stage is reached when the temperature is between 121–129°C (250–264°F) as the water evaporates from the syrup. If you dip a spoon into the syrup, the sugar will drip off the spoon in thick rope-like strands. Drop some syrup into icy water and when you remove it, a hard ball will be formed.

Icing (Confectioner's) Sugar

Icing sugar is finely powdered white sugar which dissolves instantly. Pure icing sugar has no additives, making it lumpy in texture, yet ideal for gluten-free recipes. Icing sugar mixture contains cornflour (cornstarch) as an anti-caking agent.

Iso-malt

Processed from sugar beets, iso-malt is a sugar substitute that has the same sweetness as sugar but does not bake or react in quite the same way as sugar. Commonly used in sugar-free or diabetic foods, iso-malt does not raise blood glucose levels and is considered safe for consumption by diabetics.

Jasmine Rice

The famous Thai long grain rice which has its own fragrant aroma and distinctive flavour.

Jasmine Tea

Green tea leaves are scented with fresh jasmine flowers to produce this fragrant, subtly sweet tea. A Chinese speciality for over 800 years.

Kaffir Lime Leaves

Kaffir lime leaves are high in essential oils, which give them their unique intensely refreshing citrus flavour. These leaves are used either whole or finely shredded to impart their incomparable flavour to food. The fruit of the kaffir lime tree has very little juice, but its skin makes a fragrant citrus zest to use in pastes, or as a citrus garnish.

Kitchen Blowtorch

Readily available from kitchenware stores, a butane blowtorch is an essential tool for caramelising sugar, as in crème brûlée.

Leaf Gelatine

Used as a setting agent, leaf gelatine are colourless, almost flavourless thin films of protein that form a gel when combined with liquid and heated. Leaf gelatine is softened in cold water for five minutes and squeezed gently to remove excess water before being added to recipes. Never heat gelatine to boiling point as this will stop it from setting.

Leaf gelatine comes in several different grades depending on its bloom, or firmness. They include Bronze, Silver, Gold, Platinum and Titanium. Make sure you always use the grade stated in a recipe.

Lemongrass

Lemongrass stem is packed with citral, the substance found in lemon rind, providing a zesty lemon flavour to many desserts. It's the bulb-like lower stem of the long lemongrass that is used in Asian cooking. Simply peel away the tough outer layers until you get to the pale lower stem. The stem is either used whole, slightly bruised, to infuse its flavour or is sliced very thinly crosswise, to break up its long fibres.

Light Corn Syrup
A clear, sweet syrup derived from the starch of maize. It's used to soften textures, to prevent sugar crystallisation, to avoid ice crystals in frozen desserts, and to thicken sauces and enhance flavours.

Liquid Glucose (see Glucose Syrup)

Liquid Maltose
Available from Asian supermarkets and speciality food stores, liquid maltose has been produced in China since the 2nd century BC and is the Chinese equivalent of corn syrup or liquid glucose. Made from cereal starch, which is converted to sugar by a malting process, it is very thick and sticky.

Mascarpone
A rich, thick and mild-flavoured Italian cheese made by heating cream, curdling it with citric acid, then hanging it to drain for several days.

Meringue Types
For all types of meringues, it is essential to use egg whites that are at room temperature and to make sure all your equipment is clean and free of grease which will inhibit the egg whites' ability to whip.

Three main types of meringues are:

French Meringue: fine white sugar is beaten into egg whites.

Italian Meringue: hot sugar syrup is beaten into egg whites.

Swiss Meringue: egg whites and sugar are whisked together over a saucepan of simmering water until the sugar dissolved, then the mixture is beaten.

Nutmeg
Nutmeg is the seed of an evergreen tree indigenous to Run Island in Indonesia. Mace, with its more delicate flavour, is the dried reddish covering of the nutmeg seed. Nutmeg is best used when freshly grated.

Orange Blossom Water
Orange blossom water is distilled water that contains the essential oils of the orange blossom. It adds a hint of a fragrant citrus scent to foods and complements the flavour. It's highly concentrated so only add a few drops at a time. Orange blossom water can be found at specialty food stores.

Palm Sugar: Dark vs Light
Processed from palm tree sap, the sap is boiled down in large vats until it has a thick consistency like fudge or caramel. Like sugar made from sugar cane, the colour of palm sugar indicates flavour, and it can vary from cream to almost black. Pale sugar is lovely and creamy, golden brown palm sugar has a delicious fudge-like flavour, while the very dark palm sugar has a molasses-like bitterness. Some palm sugar is sold as a soft syrup and is referred to as palm honey. Like sugar, palm sugar keeps for ages and is best stored in an airtight container.

Palm sugar is a solid lump, so with your knife, shave the sides of the sugar block, then chop the shavings. If the palm sugar is very hard it can be pounded easily in a mortar and pestle. Or place for about 30 seconds in the microwave and it will become soft and easy to chop.

Pastry Cream
A custard thickened with cornflour, its smooth and creamy texture has many uses from tart fillings to soufflé bases.

Pâté À Bombe
The French term for the base mixture used in mousse desserts. It is made by pouring 'hard ball'

sugar syrup over egg yolks and whipping the mixture until it is completely cold and forms a light, foamy mass.

Puff Pastry
A very light pastry made in layers that expand when cooked, leaving large air pockets inside, which results in a buttery, flaky pastry.

Puffed Rice
Rice grains are heated under pressure which causes them to puff up.

Rice Flour
Ground from short grain rice, rice flour has a fine light texture and is commonly used in noodles and pastries.

Rice Vinegar
Made from fermented rice, this vinegar is commonly used in China, Japan and Korea. Do not substitute with white wine vinegar as it will alter the flavour of the dish because rice vinegar is much milder and sweeter.

Sea Salt
Pure salt flakes extracted from seawater by a process of evaporation.

Sesame Seeds
Native to Africa, the sesame plant produces edible seeds rich in vitamins and minerals. With a rich, nutty flavour and an extremely high oil content, the seeds are commonly used whole by bakeries—most of Mexico's sesame crop is purchased by McDonald's for their sesame seed buns.

Star Anise
A star-shaped pod from the flower of a North Vietnam tree, star anise has a sweet and very aromatic anise flavour. It contains the ingredient anethole which gives the sweet and very aromatic anise flavour. Star anise combines very well with chocolate.

Sugar Thermometer
A vital tool in candy making which measures temperatures up to 204°C (400°F) in order to gauge the consistency of the sugar syrup. The thermometer hangs on the inside of the pan while the sugar syrup is heating.

Szechwan Pepper
Not a true pepper, szechwan peppers are the seed casings of the Prickly Ash which grow wild in China. They have a peculiar numbing effect on the tongue and are indispensable in Chinese cuisine. Buy the peppercorns whole and store in an airtight container.

Tamarind
Tamarind comes from the bean-like pod of the tamarind tree which originated in Sudan and has a unique sweet/sour taste. The pod-like fruit contains a soft acidic pulp that is used as a spice. Buy tamarind pulp in blocks from supermarkets. Keeps for months stored in an airtight container.

Tapioca
A gluten-free starch extracted from the root of cassava, tapioca is used worldwide as a thickening agent in food. Native to Brazil, it was spread throughout the world by Portuguese and Spanish explorers.

Titanium Gelatine
All leaf gelatine is graded and titanium is one of the higher grades. Never substitute any leaf gelatine with powdered gelatine. See also Leaf Gelatine.

Turmeric

Because of its yellow colour, turmeric is used as a cheap substitute for saffron. Related to the ginger family, the bright orange rhizomes can be purchased fresh at good supermarkets. If buying ground turmeric, only purchase a small quantity as it turns 'musty' very quickly.

Vanilla Bean

The vanilla pod is the fruit of a climbing orchid that grows wild in South America and was used by the Aztecs to flavour chocolate. It was taken to Europe by the Spaniards. Each pod holds a number of tiny black seeds, which contain the flavour. The pods are picked unripened, then cured over a long process that develops their unique flavour. In the wild, vanilla is pollinated by only one species of bee and one species of hummingbird; commercial crops are usually hand-pollinated, which is one of the reasons for vanilla's high price. Store vanilla beans in a canister of caster sugar for a constant supply of vanilla sugar. Add a whole bean to fruits when poaching in wine.

Whipping Cream

Chilling cream before whipping it will reduce the chance of it curdling. Always whip cream just before you need to use it.

Ribbon stage: when the whisk is lifted you can see a ribbon trail in the cream.

Soft peak stage: the cream holds very soft peaks when the whisk is lifted.

Zest

Zest is the coloured part of the rind of citrus fruits. The underlying white pith is bitter and should be avoided. Zest can be removed with a grater, vegetable peeler or zester, depending on the recipe.

ABOUT THE CHEFS

LIBBY BOTT

Since setting off on my first backpacking holiday to Thailand in the mid-nineties, my passion for travel and discovering new cultures and cuisines has grown extensively. Enjoying festivities, immersing myself in local markets and sampling a wide range of street foods across Asia, Europe and North America has broadened my appreciation of the different traditions, flavours and cooking styles. Back home, I source fresh seasonal ingredients from our community markets, unique gourmet shops and my own backyard.

The desserts I have created for this cookbook are very personal, evolving from the ingredients, tastes and textures that I love to eat. For me, cooking is not only about the dish, it is about the way food unites us, especially the shared moments eating with friends and family. I am very fortunate to be able to extend this passion professionally and to be a part of the Spirit House team.

NADINE GUIDI

Coming from a European background, I developed a passion for delicious food at an early age and travelling to Europe triggered my passion even more. Staying with Italian relatives whose culinary skills had been passed down from generation to generation, to experience their love and joy of cooking, was an absolute delight to me. Watching the Nonnas roll out their pasta dough with a flick of the rolling pin, cutting ever so finely into hair-like pasta, picking the freshest of tomatoes from their garden for the sauce, and of course, using the best local cheese money could buy ... bellissima! I was hooked.

My formal chef training started with the compulsory French cooking techniques, working and learning from French chefs and quickly progressed into Italian cooking. Then the big step, opening my own restaurant. On my nights off, I was a regular at the local Thai restaurant and I became hooked on the freshness of Thai cuisine and its different tastes, textures and flavours. Passion for food in the Italian family is well known. That passion for me is contagious and it has spilled over into different cuisines, especially Thai.

NATHAN LASTAVEC

As a youngster, I grew up surrounded by farms, so I have fond memories of playing around the neighbourhood, snacking on the fruit and vegetables which are produced there in abundance. This childhood, along with my extended Croatian family, certainly shaped my appreciation of fresh produce and my enjoyment of sharing food with friends and family.

As a chef, I do get upset with people expecting to buy fresh produce all the year around, regardless of its seasonability. I strongly believe we should only use produce that is in season and is, whenever possible, locally sourced. The resulting flavours speak for themselves.

I hope you enjoy the recipes in this book. Remember that many are base recipes, so use them as guides to create your own variations or dinner party masterpieces. Don't be deterred if the recipes don't always work the first time—motivation to improve is what keeps professional chefs coming back to their stoves each day, the continual striving to perfect a dish.

RENEE KENNIWELL

Apprenticed to a restaurant, I was very fortunate to have chef mentors who inspired me to travel and learn. Once qualified, I headed north, working at various restaurants along the way, until I reached the beautiful tropics, where I spent some years cooking and mixing with people who shared my passion for food.

When my family started to grow, I joined the kitchen staff at Spirit House. Apart from cooking with my work colleagues, I'm happiest when I'm at home with my kids, sharing and teaching them my love of food. We often go to the local famers' markets, not just to buy fresh produce, but also to buy plants for our home vegetable garden. My favourite food times are when I let the kids use their imagination in the kitchen and we create something crazy and have fun together.

From left: Nathan, Nadine, Renee and Libby.

RECIPE INDEX

This paperback edition published by New Holland Publishers in 2017
First published in 2013 by New Holland Publishers
London • Sydney • Auckland

www.newhollandpublishers.com

The Chandlery, 50 Westminster Bridge Road, London SE1 7QY United Kingdom
1/66 Gibbes Street Chatswood NSW 2067 Australia
5/39 Woodside Ave, Northcote Auckland New Zealand

A catalogue record of this book is available at the British Library and at the National Library of Australia

ISBN: 9781742576169

10 9 8 7 6 5 4 3 2 1

Publisher: Fiona Schultz
Project editor: Jodi De Vantier
Designer: Kimberley Pearce
Stylist: Kelly Lord
Photographer: Acland Brierty
Recipes: Nathan Lastavec, Renee Kenniwell, Nadine Guidi and Libby Bott
Production director: James Mills-Hicks
Printer: Times International

Follow New Holland Publishers on
Facebook: www.facebook.com/NewHollandPublishers

UK £16.99
US $24.99